You can try to google e~ ble and read this book! J~ ~g ~~ entrepreneurs is so helpful, powerful and clear. I feel like she saved me hours of research and put me on the right path for writing, publishing and marketing my future book. Read it one great sitting—thanks for all the most important info to get started and be strategic when it comes to self-publishing!

— Annie Franchesci, Greatest Story Creative, author of *Permission to Try*

Jodi is as powerhouse of publishing knowledge. Her background in traditional publishing makes her affinity for self-publishing even more inspiring. If you are a creative entrepreneur, business owner, social media guru, or anyone who wants to write and publish a top-notch book, grab this book! I'm launching my first book right now and particularly enjoying the Launch section!

— Natalie Wise, author of *Happy Pretty Messy*

Jodi's book is so well written in plain English for anybody to understand. I love that it's broken down into sections that addresses writing hang ups, publishing headaches, and how to put your book in front on your ideal audience. It's perfect for the creative entrepreneur who is looking to write their own book!

— Reina Pomeroy, Reina + Co.

WRITE.

PUBLISH.

MARKET.

From Idea to Published Book:
The Entrepreneur's Blueprint

Second Edition

First edition 2016

www.jodibrandoneditorial.com
hello@jodibrandoneditorial.com

ISBN 978-0-9980521-1-3
Printed in the United States of America

Disclaimer
This book is designed to provide information on writing, publishing, marketing, promoting, and distributing books. It is sold with the understanding that the publisher and author are not engaged in rendering legal, accounting, or other professional services. Due to rapid changes in the book publishing industry, this book contains information on writing, publishing, and marketing as of press time. Therefore, this text should be used only as a general guide.

Contents

Introduction

Perhaps you're familiar with the statistic, from a now-famous *New York Times* study, that 81% of Americans want to write a book—but only 1% do. Don't let this be you! So many creative business owners and entrepreneurs have "write a book" on their bucket list but are intimidated by the process. If you're among them, the book publishing world is likely foreign to you (and rightfully so). You just need to know what to do, and when. In *Write.Publish.Market.* I break the process into the three main steps of the process from start to finish. When most people talk about the writing process, they're referring to these five stages:

- Prewriting,
- Drafting,
- Revising,
- Editing, and
- Publishing

Part I: Write covers prewriting, drafting, and revising. We'll work through identifying your goals for your book, identifying your topic and ideal audience, establishing the structure and outline, and creating the book's content. **Part II: Publish** covers all aspects of manuscript preparation, including editing, book design (interior and cover), and getting your book published, whether in print, ebook, or audio format. Finally, **Part III: Market** covers all aspects of book marketing, from creating a launch plan to building buzz before publication to releasing your book on launch day and keeping it top of mind long after.

You might be wondering why I advocate for entrepreneurs to self-publish rather than publish traditionally. Among the biggest two reasons are control and money.

- When you self-publish, you *control* the entire process: the time line, who works on your book (your editor, your cover designer, your interior designer, your publicist, etc.), the content, and the cover.
- When you self-publish, you keep more *money*. Traditional book publishing contracts favor the publisher, not the author. Simple as that. In *Book the Business,* authors Adam Witty and Dan Kennedy discuss the "invisible income streams" that a book can provide in the form of lead generation, speaking engagements, and referrals. For entrepreneurs, these income streams cannot be overlooked.

Book publishers today expect authors to have a platform in place before they accept a book proposal for publication. No "official" statistics exist, but the generally accepted number in the industry is 2,500. In other words, publishers expect a minimum of 2,500 book sales before they'll consider publishing a book. Where do those sales come from? Your platform. Does your platform (your email list and social media followers) indicate that you have enough fans who would purchase your book? (Note that the magic number of 2,500 isn't your total followers. It's the total number of conversions from follower to sale.) If not, a traditional book deal is unlikely, particularly with a bigger publishing house. Since many business owners want to use a book to grow their platform, they're in a catch-22. Self-publishing removes the gatekeepers. There's no publishing company to say *no*. You publish what you want and market the book however much (and in whatever capacity) you choose.

The book market is crowded. According to *Publisher's Weekly*, 695 million print and ebooks were sold in 2018. Your book must be professionally produced to be found. Each section of *Write.Publish.Market.* is equally important to the book publishing process. Let's get started.

PART I: WRITE

Chapter 1

Your Why, What, and Who: Goals, Topic, and Audience

The core pieces of the writing stage answer the questions *why*, *what*, and *who*. Your goal(s), topic, and audience provide the foundation of your book. Take the time to clarify these before you ever write your first word.

> Knowing your why is massively important.
> — Amy Landino

Your Goals

Why are you writing a book? What do you want this book to do for you and your business? The creative business owners and solopreneurs I talk with every day most often identify four reasons when starting the book-writing process:

- Credibility (AKA influence),
- Visibility,
- Growth (business leads/clients/opportunities), and
- Money.

Let's break each of these down so you can see what they might look like for you and your business.

Credibility and Visibility

Credibility and visibility aren't the same, but they work similarly as far as platform-building, and they work together to create a snowball effect for business owners. A book can help you stand out from others in your industry.

Say you are a food blogger and have a personal chef business, and your niche is party foods. You've been in the industry for about three years. You've written a couple of guest posts on a popular food magazine's blog, and the latest, about holiday open house menus, goes viral. Obviously, you already have some credibility online because you're an established food blogger with your own library of content and growing audience. A couple of weeks after that post "gets legs," you get a phone call from a morning news show in your local community. A producer who is planning a segment on Super Bowl snacks saw your guest post and wants to feature you as the expert for their segment. You've taken your credibility and are building visibility: Not only do you have your own blog audience, but the food magazine's audience saw your post, and now you're about to add a local TV audience to your following.

Fast-forward two weeks. Your segment goes well. You receive positive feedback and had good chemistry with the show's on-air talent. Lots of new people start checking out your blog and following you on social media.

A few months later you receive an email from a producer at a *national* morning show. She saw a clip of you on the local show and needs a guest for a segment on Mother's Day tea menus. See the snowball effect? Visibility and credibility feed off of each other. All the while, you're growing your platform on your site and blog. Every time you make an appearance in print, on a blog, on a show—anywhere—you add that to your media kit and/or the "As Seen On" section of your website and in your email signature. More and more people start asking in comments on your blog posts, in emails, and on your social media accounts if you've ever thought about writing a cookbook. (Of course, you have!)

Growth

Both credibility and visibility lead to growth, which is obviously a primary goal of any business owner, you and me included. For you, this might mean more leads who develop into one-on-one clients in your signature program. It might mean speaking opportunities that put you in front of new audiences. As you try to grow your business, whatever that looks like for you, a book is one tool to do so.

A Quick Word about Money

Money might not be your primary goal, but it should certainly be *a* goal. If it wasn't, you wouldn't be spending so much time and effort (and money) writing and publishing a book, right? A book is a significant undertaking. The payoff likely won't come immediately—or it might come indirectly. Maybe the food blogger we discussed earlier lands a private dinner party with a celebrity who's in the area to shoot a movie. Her invoice from that one event likely covers all of the book-related expenses she spent publishing her book. In that case, she isn't earning the bulk of her money from book royalties, but rather from client work.

This type of scenario happens regularly with business owners who write self-development books. Someone might read a business strategist's book, for example, and decide to hire her for one-on-one work. The strategist would need to sell thousands of books to come close to earning that same amount in book royalties. Be open to what "money" looks like when mapping out your book goals.

SMART Goals

When identifying your book goals, consider the concept of SMART goals. SMART goals are:

- Specific,
- Measurable,
- Achievable,
- Relevant, and
- Time-bound.

Crafting SMART goals can be tricky with a product like a book since so many of the benefits of writing a book to serve your business are intangible. How do you measure influence, for example? You *can,* though, measure business leads, new one-on-one clients, and more. Take a look at a few examples.

Specific

If your goal is not specific, it has no urgency. This lack of urgency makes it easy to put it off or continually move it further down your priority list.

No: *I'm going to write a book.*

Yes: *I'm going to write a book this year for women who are struggling to balance their new baby with their business.*

The latter identifies the target audience for your book as well as a time frame, two elements around which you've established specificity. The more specific you are when articulating a goal, the easier it will be to visualize yourself reaching it. Surely, you've heard about successful business people and athletes talking about visualization and the impact it can have on your dreams and goals. Visualize yourself holding your finished book in your hand—and visualize your business growing as a result of the book.

Measurable

If your goals aren't measurable, you won't know when to celebrate achieving them (a concept I very much believe in).

No: *My book will be published this year.*

Yes: *My book will be published in October of this year so that I can schedule speaking engagements throughout the fall, and the book will be available for holiday promotions.*

Consider this: Just about everything *can* be measured. Other book-related examples include completing your first draft by a specific date, writing X number of words each day, achieving Amazon best-seller status, and meeting sales goals.

Good, Better, Best

A concept that's gained quite a bit of traction in the business world over the last several years is the "good, better, best" framework, which happens to work beautifully with measurable goals. Setting a sales launch goal using this framework is definitely something to consider as you create your launch plan. (See Part III.)

A *good* goal is one that's realistic and that you'll be happy to meet. A *better* goal is a stretch but still achievable (with a solid launch plan). A *best* goal is one that would knock your socks off.

Achievable

Depending on how you frame your goals, writing a book may or may not be achievable. Book writing is not necessarily a black-or-white, yes-or-no scenario. Consider what you already have on your calendar. This includes business commitments, volunteer activities, family time—anything that's already on your calendar.

No: *I can squeeze book writing into my calendar.*

Yes: *If I postpone my course launch until next spring, I can write the book in December and January, using the time I had planned to be doing course creation.*

If you've set unachievable goals and not met them (of course you haven't!), you end up feeling lousy about yourself.

Relevant

Where does a book fit into your business goals—short-term and long-term? If one of your goals is to establish yourself as an authority in your niche, then a book is likely relevant.

No: *Three colleagues are writing books.*

Yes: *A book will be a tool to help me grow the speaking arm of my business.*

If you haven't framed your goal so that it is relevant to you, it may be challenging to remain committed to it (making it unachievable, and you just read above what happens when that's the case).

Time-Bound

"Someday" is not what you're looking for here. Give yourself a deadline, but make it realistic so that it remains achievable.

No: *I will write a book next year.*

Yes: *I am launching three new products this year but will hire a book coach in November to plan and write my book next spring and launch it in September.*

The latter goal frames the process so that you are holding yourself accountable with mini deadlines along the way.

Do you see how the different elements of SMART goals work together? You set goals that are measurable *and* achievable by not overreaching. You set goals that are time-bound *and* specific so that you know what needs to be accomplished (and when).

Taking time up-front to define your goals honestly and set expectations helps you meet your goals easily.

Don't Forget Your Readers' Goals

It's not just about you! As you're setting goals for your book, remember that your audience has goals, too. What are they hoping to learn or gain by reading your book? If you stray too far from that, no matter how great your intentions are, your book won't serve the reader—and in turn, won't serve you and your business. (See the section on chapter audits in Chapter 4 to learn how to ensure you're meeting readers' needs with your book.)

Your target audience will directly affect not only how you craft your book but also how you market it.
— Katherine Pickett

Topic

Your book topic is the *what*. What are you writing about? Your industry is probably your topic area. You'll narrow it down from there to find your focused book topic.

Use Google AdWords Keyword Planner (https://adwords. google.com/KeywordPlanner) to conduct market research on your topic. Look at the "average monthly searches" column to see if your subject is too broad or too narrow. Another idea is to use Amazon's "autocompleter." Start typing in a word and see what else Amazon automatically fills in. (You can do this with Google as well.) When I type in "book writing," for example, the first two results are "book writing kit" and "book writing for dummies." That tells me the best-selling book-related books on Amazon are how-to books targeted to beginners rather than to advanced-level writers. This makes sense to me because every day I hear, "I want to write a book, but I have no idea where to start." (This is also why you're reading an overview-type book, covering the entire writing/publishing process, rather than a book covering one part of the process in further depth.)

> To produce a mighty book, you must choose a mighty theme.
> — Herman Melville

Let's start with the big-picture topic. Think about the general area where you would find the book in a bookstore or library or the category on Amazon. I ask my clients, "On what shelf will I find your book?" I'll use myself as an example. I've been working in book publishing for about 20 years. You can find this book in the book publishing/writing reference section. It wouldn't make sense for me to write a book about nutrition or marketing or even magazine publishing. The topic of this book will fit under the umbrella of book publishing, and that's reference (general) or writing/publishing reference (specific).

Amazon Categories and BISAC Codes

Think of Amazon as a search engine, like Google. This makes it easier to understand how to make your book stand out by correctly using keywords, categories, and themes.

Traditional publishing relies on the industry standard of categorizing and sorting books: BISAC, which stands for Book Industry Standards and Communications. As of March 2019, there are 51 main categories that break into 4,498 sub-categories. (If you're feeling book nerdy, these are available on the Book Industry Study Group website. See the Resources.) Amazon, though, uses its search engine to determine categories based on what customers are looking for (AKA consumer demand). Be sure to monitor Amazon's categories, as new categories appear regularly and you might want to adjust yours (for example, a new category might more closely align with your book topic).

When you list a book on Amazon, you're allowed to choose two categories. The trick is to choose the Amazon category that most resembles the BISAC category you want to reach.

Amazon calls sub-categories themes. For example,

> when you search for "writing" in the Books area on Amazon, on the left side, you can narrow your search by writing skill reference, fiction writing reference, writing reference, grammar reference, authors, and more.
>
> Selecting the right categories for your book takes some legwork, but taking this time is so important. (Readers can't buy what they can't find.) Once you have a few books similar to yours, look at each one's categories and sub-categories.

Where's Your Expertise?

What's your zone of genius? Or, put another way, what is your area of expertise? This exercise will be somewhat familiar to readers who host a Facebook group or page, have an email list, or have a blog. What are the questions that you hear regularly? These are the areas in which your audience already sees you as an expert. Capitalize on that! Give them what they want. They're turning to you as an expert in this field, whatever it may be. They see you as someone trustworthy and credible— someone who can answer their questions.

Think about your elevator pitch—that 30-second introduction you share when you first meet someone at a networking event or are introduced to someone at a cocktail party. Or the way you introduce yourself on Facebook Live, Instagram Live, or a webinar or masterclass. You might have heard me say, for example, "For those of you who don't know me, I'm Jodi Brandon. I'm a book writing coach, editor, and publishing consultant for creative entrepreneurs and small business owners who want to use a book to help market their business. I teach you the language of the book publishing world." The questions I get most frequently are about book publishing and book editing and writing.

The general, overarching theme in that elevator speech is the general topic that your book probably falls under. It gets more specific, though. It wouldn't make sense for me to say, "My book is about publishing." If I were writing *Book Publishing 101,* that book could be 1,000 pages long. I'm not interested in writing that book, so I narrowed the subject down. And if there are multiple topic areas, maybe you have multiple books in your future. A great way to build your platform is to use a book as a springboard for another book and then another book (but that's a different book, pun intended).

The key here is that to write about something outside your area of expertise could be likened to swimming upstream: possible, but so much harder. You already have so much knowledge on your topic—and you know who to talk to and where to find the rest.

Audience

Who are you writing for? Who are your readers? Before you can write for an audience, you need to determine who that is. As a business owner, you know that you cannot serve everyone. You need a niche. You need an ideal client or clients. The same is true of your book: You can't write for everyone. If you try, your message will end up diluted. So you must determine and be clear about who you're writing for.

When you write to everyone, you write to no one.
— Rachel Stout

I suspect that most of you reading this book have done the exercise in your businesses in which you've created your ideal client avatar by asking all sorts of questions. Is this person male or female? How old is this person? What does this person do for a living? How much money does he or she make? (This helps determine purchasing power.) Where does she live? All of these questions help clarify who your ideal client is. Many business owners name that person. I use a couple in my business, one of whom is Amy. Amy is a real-life friend of mine who's a blogger. Amy says that, until she met me, she never in a million years thought that she would write a book, and now she actually thinks she could do it one day. Sometimes when I talk to Amy (and others), I fall back on my history in book publishing and publishing industry lingo. Amy stops me and says, "Jodi, I don't know what the heck that word means. Talk to Amy." These conversations with Amy have changed the way I interact with clients, explain processes to them, and educate them on the book publishing process. (Hi, Amy, if you're reading this!)

To determine your ideal book audience, take the ideal client exercise a step further. Think about where this person is reading your book. On an airplane on the way to a business conference? In the school pickup line? Maybe she's a mompreneur who is trying to fit in business in between shuffling the kids from here to there, picking them up from school and getting them to soccer practice. Is this person reading a couple of chapters here and there during 30-minute elliptical workouts? Visualize where this person is reading your book.

Also, think about what the book looks like. Is he or she reading on an iPad? Or is it a physical book? Is it a hardback book? Is it a paperback book? Is it large? Is it small? Maybe she's listening to an audio version of your book. The more specific you can get this image in your head, the more excited you can get about it.

Secondary Audiences

In addition to the primary audience for your book, there are likely secondary audiences who will benefit from reading it. I recently worked with a pelvic health expert on her book. The primary audience was, naturally, women looking for a better understanding of their bodies. In her introduction, though, she spelled out the various secondary audiences for her book: partners of women, women's healthcare practitioners, service providers like yoga instructors, and more. So smart!

Take the time to figure out who *your* "Amy" is and who your secondary audiences are. Knowing who these people are will guide you throughout the writing, publishing, and marketing processes.

Action Steps

Without knowing your destination, it's difficult to forge a path to reach it. The elements in this chapter—your goals, topic, and audience—pave that path.

Determine:

- Your goals and your audience's goals (**why**),
- Your book topic (**what**), and
- Your audience(s) (**who**).

Chapter 2
A Writer's Mindset: Fears and Roadblocks

So much writing advice is meant for professional writers, and that's not your goal. You aren't looking to perfect a craft or even write multiple books. To write a book to serve your business, though—which *is* your goal—requires a writer's mindset.

I wish that there was a secret answer to answer the question "How can I make myself believe that I'm a real writer and not a business owner writing a book?" Unfortunately, there's no secret formula. There's no secret sauce. There's no secret anything. It's a matter of shifting your mindset from business owner to writer. You must convince yourself that you can be a writer—if only for a season. This chapter breaks down fears and obstacles, the two most significant (and, frankly, common) impediments to making that mindset shift.

Fears: Defining and Overcoming Them

Fear gets in our way, particularly when it comes to something on our bucket list or a "someday" project. Every author, whether first-time or experienced (professional writers included), has fears around writing. So many things can hold us back from not just writing a book but doing all sorts of things. Especially for people who don't consider themselves trained professional writers, fears often stop them from writing a book. Or worse, they do write it but then keep the manuscript stored on a computer somewhere rather than publishing it.

The fears my clients most often identify when it comes to book writing will likely sound familiar to you. Fear of rejection, fear of failure, fear of success, perfectionism (that's me), impostor syndrome, analysis paralysis, overthinking everything, avoidance—do any of these ring a bell? Regardless of your fear or fears, the process to overcome looks similar: identify them, acknowledge that they exist, and try to figure out how they came to be such a driving force in your life. With a root cause, it will be easier to recognize when they are showing up and preventing you from moving forward. Then you can work to overcome them so you *can* move forward—in this case, with a writing project.

Let's break down a couple of these fears in a little more detail.

My perfectionism started when I attended Catholic elementary school. One day my fourth-grade classmates and I had to identify what we wanted to be when we grew up. I said that I wanted to "work with words." I didn't know at that point what a book editor was or what an English major was. I just knew that I loved reading, and I loved writing. I had a diary with one of those little keys that I thought would keep my brother out of it. (Didn't work!) I was constantly rewriting my notes in school because I hated to make mistakes.

My teacher, Sister Frances, regularly told me—that day and for the remainder of the school year—that I would never "work with words" when I grew up because I was not earning 100% on my English tests (never mind that I was getting 95% and 98%). Her words *really* stuck with me.

Whenever I feel myself getting frustrated with myself (*How could you not catch that mistake, Jodi?*), I tell myself that pencils have erasers for a reason: because nobody is perfect. I keep this written on a sticky note on my desk because it's a good way for me to mentally reset myself. (*Nobody's perfect. Do not let perfectionism take over. Just keep moving forward.*) It's a mindset shift.

> Don't let perfection become procrastination.
> — Danielle LaPorte

Rejection is a big fear when it comes to book writing and publishing. What if no one buys the book? What if people hate it and leave bad reviews? Consider these stories from the annals of traditional publishing:

- Stephen King's *Carrie* was rejected 30 times before it was published.
- Jack Canfield's *Chicken Soup for the Soul* anthology was rejected 140 times. Publisher after publisher told Canfield that anthologies don't sell. One hundred and twenty-five million-plus copies of that original book later, there are dozens of spinoff and ancillary books and products.
- J.K. Rowling's *Harry Potter* was rejected 12 times. (I'll bet those decision-makers have kicked themselves just a few times.)

Once you've identified your fears, you can work through them to actually move forward and make progress rather than feeling stuck.

First consider, when something specific is bothering you, its magnitude. Is it a big thing or a small thing? If it's a small thing, give yourself a little more latitude, and understand that everybody's going to make mistakes. With bigger issues, give yourself some time to think about it—but also give yourself a time limit. If you're deciding between title A and title B, think about it for a day or two, and then decide. If you're trying to decide whether to include an interview with someone in the book, consider the pros and cons. Maybe this person has sold a million books but recently said something in an interview that rubbed you the wrong way. This decision has a potentially significant impact if this is a well-known person who could lend credence to your book. Give yourself several days, or maybe even a week, to think about it. You don't want to rush to a decision, but you walk the line of avoidance and staying stuck.

Next, make a list of all of your options. What are all of the possible solutions that you could do to solve problem X? Go through this list to eliminate options that would be logistically difficult or that don't quite fit. You're then left with better options to choose from. This process is similar in a way to the brain dump exercise you'll do in Chapter 3. Just get it all down, and then regroup.

Have a couple of people you can go to for feedback when you're stuck on something or when you're trying to decide between two options. I caution you here not to have too many outside voices coming in because then it's easy to stay stuck. (*Well, Pat thinks this, but Anne thinks this, and I really value both of their opinions equally, so now I just don't know what to do, so maybe I'll wait a little bit longer to decide. Or maybe I should ask Eileen and Kathy to weigh in, too.*) Don't do that. Instead, seek opinions only from people whom you trust—and who know what you're working on, understand how you think, and can help you work through a problem rather than just throwing another opinion or layer of the information into the mix.

This process can help you overcome many fears, but especially analysis paralysis, overthinking, fear of failure, avoidance, and fear of the unknown.

Let's also touch on impostor syndrome, something many business owners deal with as they enter the book publishing world. (*Who am I to be writing a book? I'm a strategist, not a writer. I'm a photographer, not a writer. I'm a business coach, not a writer. I'm a food blogger, not a writer.*) We all have knowledge to share. You have knowledge and a story that other strategists don't have, that other photographers don't have, that other coaches don't have, that other food bloggers don't have. Whatever your niche, you have a unique angle on that subject area—and you have your own story to share and book to write. When this fear creeps in, think back to the ideal reader profile you identified in Chapter 1. For whom are you writing? These readers will pick up your book because they see you as an expert. They see you as an expert because you're providing value to them. Shift the focus away from you (*I'm not qualified. I am not a writer.*) and onto those readers. Think about the value and the information you're providing to them. You're not an imposter to them; you're the expert. That's why they're coming to you with their questions right now, on your blog, your email list, your Facebook page, and Instagram. That's why you are the expert writing this book.

I find that having a mantra to reset yourself when fear creeps in is helpful. When my perfectionist tendencies reveal themselves, I remind myself: Pencils have erasers for a reason.

Roadblocks

All writers face roadblocks, not just you. (I know it feels that way sometimes.) Hurdles get in our way and slow us down. Knowing how to face these head-on and giving yourself some grace in dealing with roadblocks help.

The four obstacles I hear the most about from my book writing clients (all of which I've faced, too) are:
- Creative lapse (a fancy way of saying writer's block),
- Self-doubt (*Where did my muse go? Where's my mojo?*),
- Burnout, and
- Self-sabotage (AKA ugly inner critic).

A lot of writing advice boils down to "It doesn't matter what's going on. Sit your butt in the chair and get the words written. If your goal is to write 1,000 words, then sit there until you write 1,000 words." That sounds great in theory, but that's not always realistic. Hear me: I'm **not** saying that you shut down your computer at the first sign of "Oh, I don't know what word to write next. I guess I'm done for the day." No. There's a happy medium there.

Creative Lapse

Writing is like a muscle. The more you use that muscle, the stronger it's going to be. Essentially, you can (and need to) train your brain to write. Perhaps you've heard the phrase *use it or lose it*? If you don't use a muscle, it will atrophy. So writing is not just about being a good reader and deciding you want to write. You have to write. You have to practice writing. Write every day. Find a website with writing prompts if you don't want to free-write. This will give you the confidence to know that you *can* write.

Self-Doubt

The bottom line here is we have to get out of our own way. We are our biggest obstacles a lot of the time, unfortunately. Especially in a situation like book-writing—in which entrepreneurs feel out of our element—we feel like impostors. We feel like a "real" writer wouldn't get stuck or not know what to write next, for example. Take it from someone who's worked with many such people: That's not necessarily the case. Remember that you have knowledge to share and value to provide. Again, shift your thinking: Think about your audience and what you're providing to them.

I regularly hear from book coaching clients that their writing is terrible. They doubt whether they have an entire book in them. This is true for all humans, not just those writing a book. We doubt ourselves. We doubt our ability. But know this: *Everybody's* first draft stinks. You can edit bad writing. You can improve writing that you think is bad (but probably isn't that bad). You cannot improve a blank page. You cannot edit a blank page. You cannot publish a blank page. You can't do anything until those words are written.

> The worst enemy to creativity is self-doubt.
> — Sylvia Plath

Burnout

Entrepreneurs know burnout. In fact, we're prone to burnout. We work too hard, we sneak into our offices after our families are long asleep, and we check our phones before our feet even hit the floor in the morning. We have so many ideas, and a lot of us are control freaks. So, we know burnout.

When you think about writing a book, remember that you're still running a business. Trying to fit writing a book into an already-busy schedule and add one more thing to the list doesn't work.

You need a solid plan for getting your book researched, written, and published—but that plan needs to be realistic for your life. You've seen, I'm sure, writing programs that promise a book in a month or 30 days or a weekend. I caution you to consider the often-unrealistic expectations some of those programs set up for people.

> It is more important to know where you are going than to get there quickly.
> — Mabel Newcomber

Realistic expectations and then managing those expectations are the way to combat burnout when it comes to book writing. A short time frame like a week or a weekend may work for a 15,000-word book or ebook manuscript, but probably not for a 40,000- or 50,000-word book manuscript.

Self-Sabotage

We're all good at criticizing ourselves. I encourage you instead to treat yourself and your writing the way you would treat someone else and someone else's writing. Give yourself a bit of grace. Understand where there's room for improvement (and there always is), but don't be overly critical of yourself. That feeds into the fears you identified earlier in the chapter. I want you to move forward on the path to published author, not stuck at a standstill.

How, exactly, do we get out of our own way and deal with these roadblocks (creative lapse, self-doubt, burnout, and self-sabotage)? Take a break. You need to reset your brain. This advice is definitely not rocket science, but sometimes we just need to hear someone else say it. Take a 10-minute break. Take a walk around the block. Sometimes you just need a change of scenery. Take your laptop to your local coffee shop. Go to the library, if you need quiet or if you don't like noise. Sometimes a simple change of scenery is all you need. Even within your own house, if you can't get out, move to a different space or room. Play with your pet for a few minutes. Sometimes it really is that simple. If all else fails, have a dance party for a few minutes.

Your goal? Give your brain a chance to reset itself. After that, yes, it's time for "butt in chair." Sit down and try to write. If you give it a few more minutes and still nothing happens, then I say call it a day and adjust your writing schedule (which you'll read more about in the next chapter). Things happen. Life happens. Sometimes a circumstance like a family emergency or an illness prevents you from writing that day; sometimes it's one of the roadblocks outlined in this chapter. That doesn't make you a bad writer, and that doesn't mean you won't finish your book; it just means you're having a bad day. Do not force creativity. It's counter-productive to try. Reset your brain, give it a rest, and try again tomorrow.

Action Steps

As an entrepreneur, you need to temporarily adopt a writer's mindset. Be aware of common fears and roadblocks that affect all writers (professional or not).

- Determine what fear(s) you have around writing and develop a mantra to face them head-on.
- Be wary of common roadblocks so you can stay out of your own way.

Chapter 3

Prewriting

Prewriting is separate from writing. I cannot emphasize that strongly enough. If you sit down to write a 50,000-word book with nothing but a topic and a few key points, you're in trouble. Prewriting is the legwork and preparation to make the actual writing easier and faster. Trying to do both tasks at once will make you want to pull out your hair (let alone finish writing your book!). This chapter breaks down the prewriting phase so you can set yourself up for writing success.

Structure Your Book: Brain Dump

A lot of people hate the "o word" (outline)—especially creative and online entrepreneurs. We feel it's constricting. We feel it's too structured, too buttoned-up, too formal. (I say "we" because I'm one of those people who dreaded outlining in school and put it off as long as humanly possible.) Yet we need to get our ideas organized before we start writing a book. Can you "wing it" with a 1,000-word blog post? Sure. But a 40,000-word book? Not so much.

Enter the brain dump. Non-restrictive, non-threatening—fluid even. Brain dumping is the anti-outline and *almost* makes idea formation a fun process rather than a task we have to check off of our list.

Please note: If you are an outliner, then, by all means, create an outline rather than doing a traditional brain dump! In my 20-ish years' experience with book authors, though, I've met only a handful of you.

Everybody knows what the brain dump is. Some people call it mind mapping; it has lots of different names. To brain dump, you need a pen or a pencil, a timer, and a piece of paper. That's it! The key is to pick the right amount of time. I like the three- to five-minute range. You want a long enough time to get into a groove (you might, for those first 10 or 15 seconds, just sit there thinking, *Oh my gosh, I can't think of anything to write down.*), but not so much time that you run out of things. Looking at the timer and still having three or four minutes left is discouraging.

With a brain dump, you are tricking your mind into working in the short time frame that you set. If you set the timer for three minutes and have more ideas when the timer goes off, no problem, set the timer for three minutes again, and keep going. When you're finished, look at your paper and take in what you've recorded. You'll start to see where topics/phrases/ideas could be grouped together. Do another brain dump later (maybe an hour or maybe a day or two later) and add to the first one. Surely you didn't think of everything related to your topic the first time.

A brain dump is never truly "finished," whereas sometimes when we delete or re-order material on an outline, it feels like we made a mistake. The brain dump is meant to be fluid: You're *meant* to move words and phrases, so that like items are near like items on the page. You're *meant* to scratch off something here and move other words elsewhere on the paper, or circle a concept and "move it" with a big arrow to somewhere else on the page. By the time you're ready to start writing, your brain dump looks like a big mess, and that's how it's supposed to be. The idea is that it can change and evolve throughout the writing process as you figure out exactly how you're going to organize your book.

Once you do a brain dump on the general topic you identified in Chapter 1, take it deeper. Pull out an idea or two and do another brain dump just on that idea (a micro brain dump). As you do more of these, you're essentially creating a working table of contents for your book.

Let's take my first book, *Become a Book Editor*, as an example. My initial brain dump gave me general ideas: types of editors, editing skills that you need, where to work. I took each of those and did a brain dump of just that. "Where to work" then included general book publishers, literary agencies, book packagers, and independent publishers. Then I went deeper with yet another brain dump.

Instead of including those broad places to work, I listed big publishers, small publishers, niche publishers, general book packagers, niche packagers, and specialty literary agencies.

The idea is to keep narrowing down the topic. "Where to Work" became a chapter in *Become a Book Editor*, and that chapter was divided into parts: publishers, big publishers, small publishers, niche publishers. My brain dumps outlined the book for me; it just didn't *look like* an outline. When you have a creative mind, you want to feel like you're in control of the process as much as possible.

Hopefully, you start to see your book structure and your book contents coming alive as you brain dump, which is the goal. And remember that it's a *working* table of contents. You will make changes as you get into the thick of writing and revising, but you at least have the seedling to work from as you start thinking about the next phase (research).

How Many Words?

It's frustrating to hear that there is no "perfect" word count target for your book. (You're probably thinking, *How can I create a writing schedule or figure out how long it will take if I don't know how many words I need?*) "Enough words to cover your topic" sounds like the kind of smart-aleck answer that would've gotten me in trouble in high school. But it's true.

That said, I can provide a few guidelines. The two most common trim sizes for trade nonfiction books are 5x8 and 6x9 inches. Think about which size you prefer, since you'll choose for yourself. For the larger, 6x9 trim size, you're looking at about 250 words per page, according to the Nonfiction Authors Association. These books are generally heftier in general, so for a 150-page book, you can target 37,500 words and 50,000 words for a 200-page book. The 5x8 trim size means about 200 words per page; too many more than that and you need a smaller, less-readable font in a print book. A 100-page book would be, then, about 20,000 words; a 150-page book would be roughly 30,000 words. These numbers are averages, of course, and depend on margins, font choice, and graphics/images, among other factors.

The a-ha moment with regard to book size often comes when you physically look at some books on your shelf or at a bookstore. On a recent (video) coaching call with a client, she was examining books on her office bookshelf. She picked up a book that was 5x8 inches and about 120 pages. Her first thought? "Oh, wow—it feels like there's nothing to it. I want my book to feel heftier than this." To an author-entrepreneur, this "feel" is just as important as writing a book within the same *general* word count as others in your genre. Novels are 100K-plus words, for example, not business and personal development books. The average nonfiction book length is 50,000 words, with some differentiation based on your specific genre within the nonfiction category.

> Put one word after another.
> — Neil Gaiman

Also keep in mind that other trim sizes are available but are often considered "custom" by printing companies, which will increase your cost per book (which you'll pass on to readers). Depending on your genre, though, a different trim size might make more sense. A photography book, for example, lends itself to a larger format in part for the "WOW" factor one gets from large photos (especially color photos!).

Repurposing Existing Content
Don't let these high word-count averages scare you. As an author-entrepreneur, you already have plenty of content that you can repurpose for your book. Think about the following sources to get your wheels turning;

there are many more:

- Blog posts,
- Podcast interviews,
- Webinars/masterclasses,
- Email newsletters,
- Articles,
- Videos, and
- Guest posts.

Organizing content to be repurposed can be tricky. There's more to it than cutting and pasting old blog posts into a Word document and calling that a book manuscript. You'll need to update text, add transition text between new and old material, and the like. Think of repurposing as a way to jump-start your book draft. Imagine how good it will feel to have several thousand words in your total word count before you even begin writing new material.

Research

Once you see what you have, by organizing your content bank to see what can be repurposed, you'll know what you still need. That's where research comes in.

If you sit down to write your book without doing any re-search, your first draft will be just a shell of a manuscript. You'll have a few sentences here, and then a highlight on the computer screen where you typed "Look up statistic about marketing here." You'll have all sorts of holes like that throughout your manuscript, which will be depressing when you go to re-vise. Why? Your draft isn't really a complete, workable draft at all. If you, instead, create a research plan before you even start writing, then when it comes time to actually write, and you need to fill in that missing statistic, you have it.

You can, for example, insert that statistic right into the manuscript and keep writing—no need to return to that section later. Your research includes interviews as well as basic research like you did in high school, in college, and even in middle school: looking up sources, taking notes, lots and lots of reading. My husband teases me that I "use reading as advice for everything" to our nieces and my nephews. Guilty. I'm constantly telling them to read, read, read. You just never know when you're going to come across a snippet of information or a quote that might work in something you're writing.

Read anything you can get your hands on. Google is your best friend as a writer. (Hopefully, you can file this under "I already know that, Jodi": Wikipedia is *not* your best friend as a writer since anyone can change things on Wikipedia.)

Interviews

Think about people in your industry you'd like to talk to. You may or may not know these people. If you don't, maybe one of your biz besties does and can introduce you via email. These are people who are established in your industry—people whose words can lend credence to what you're trying to say. Let's say, for example, you are a lifestyle blogger writing a book about some of the events that you've styled. Your dream interview is Joanna Gaines of HGTV fame.

You wouldn't email Joanna on Tuesday morning and say, "Hey, I'm writing a book about styling events. I would love to interview you for my book. Can you call me this afternoon?" That's not the right approach when you're approaching someone from whom you're seeking a favor (their time and expertise). Certainly, you want to give the interviewee the choice of time, but you shouldn't expect the person to have same-day, or maybe even same-week availability. (That's another reason to plan ahead. You don't want to be ready to write but have interviews that haven't even been conducted yet.)

Think about your wish list of interviewees and plan back-ups in case they're not available, not available in your time frame, or not interested (sorry to say this *does* sometimes happen).

I reread a great tip recently from mystery writer Chris Well on a writing blog. He was speaking about interviewing people for fiction books, but this tip applies to nonfiction books, too. Chris says to write down all the questions you want to ask this particular source and then cross out the ones that you could ask anybody. You're left with things that *only* this person can talk about. In our example, you want to ask Joanna Gaines questions that she can talk about, but other style bloggers can't speak to. I wish I would have seen that advice 10–15 years ago, but I've implemented this tip in my writing since first reading it. Instead of asking everybody the same questions, focus on the expertise they can share with you—and that you can then share with your audience. So smart.

You might call people who you've worked with in the past, let them know you're writing a book, and ask for a bit of their time to discuss topic ABC. Some of them will say *yes*, some will say *no*, and some might say *yes* if you keep it anonymous. If you think you need to use names, cross them off your list and call your backup person.

The other type of interviews you might do are with current and/or past clients. Many author-entrepreneurs write books that involve case studies, and our clients are often the perfect people to use for this information. They're likely to say *yes*, for one, because they already know and trust us. A book writing client of mine recently decided to add a case study–type profile to each chapter of her book. She hosts a podcast, so I asked if any of her podcast guests might be a good fit. We reviewed her episode list and realized that she could fit all but two of her chapter topics by using podcast transcripts (with permission from the guests, of course). Oftentimes you'll need or want to change names and/or identifying information, but your client roster is an invaluable resource when book writing.

Top 5 Interview Do's
1. Keep the interview professional, even if the interviewee is a friend.
2. Don't misquote the interviewee.
3. Be respectful of the interviewee's time. If you ask for 15 minutes, don't take more than 15 minutes.
4. Thank the interviewee.
5. Send a copy of the book to the interviewee when it's released with a note thanking them again.

Reading, Listening, and Taking Notes

Aside from interviewing experts for quotations for your book and background, the other type of research you'll do involves reading, listening, and taking notes. Read blogs, read books, listen to podcasts, listen to audiobooks, read the newspaper, read industry magazines. As I mentioned previously, you never know when you will come across a piece of information that you might be able to use in your book, or even that might spark an idea that makes you think, *Ooh, I want to talk to that person* or *That's a great idea for me to mention when I'm talking about X, Y, Z.* Any relevant piece of information you come across could become a sub-topic or a section of your book.

The key to remember when you're reading and listening is documentation. You don't always know in advance what will make it into the book and what won't. What if you decide you want to use a quotation and you have no idea where it came from? Did you hear it on a podcast? Whose? Did you read it on a blog? Is it from a book? We're all on information overload, so don't count on being able to remember where something came from if you didn't document it at the time you heard or read it.

Taking notes on your book is not the same as writing the first draft.
— Monica Leonelle

Keep track of as much information about a source as you can so you have it later if you need it. If it's a book, you want the author, title, publisher, publication date, and even page number if possible. If it's a podcast, you want the name of the podcast, episode title, guest name, host name, date the podcast was released or recorded, and link to the episode. I'm not suggesting your book will be filled with endnotes (most of us are not writing the type of academic, formal books that need endnotes), but you still need to credit your sources. If you want to use a quote that so-and-so said on a podcast, say that in your text: "As so-and-so said on the XYZ podcast on May 1, 2019" before the quote. That's enough for most sources. You want to provide readers with enough information to track down a source if they want to. (We'll talk more about permissions later in the chapter, but for now, remember this: The easier you can make it on yourself, the better.)

If you end up with more sources than you need or use, consider adding a bibliography or resources section to your book. Readers love this type of "extra," so why not provide one?

Permissions and Copyright

Copyright law is tricky because it's a gray area. There's no "This is the rule. This is always the rule no matter what." That, in turn, makes permissions tricky—and can make authors nervous. Remember that I am not a lawyer, copyright or otherwise. What I know from working with authors for 20 years, writing books myself, and even editing a book on copyright (swear it's true!) is that what we—all of us in the book publishing world—need to be worried about with copyright law is fair use. Fair use has four factors:

- Nature of the use,
- Purpose of the use,
- Amount of the use, and
- Effect of the use.

Authors really need to be concerned with two of those: the purpose and the amount. What are you doing with this work that you're using/quoting from? Are you using it to educate your audience, to emphasize your point, or to offer another varying perspective? Those fall under the idea of educating your audience, which is typically fine. That's the *purpose*.

As far as *amount*, think of it this way: Using 50 words of a

1,000-word article is 5%. Using 50 words of a 200-word poem is 25%. Huge difference, right? I would bet that that poet is not happy that someone is using 25% of his or her work without permission (or compensation). You need to consider those two factors—purpose and amount—together.

Hard and fast rules would make copyright law so much easier and so much more enjoyable to try to figure out, but, unfortunately, that's not the case. Publishers have their own guidelines. A publisher might tell its author, "You may not use more than X number of words without permission." At that point, the author needs to either reduce the quoted material to that many words or replace it with something different—paraphrase that excerpt.

Every publisher has its own rules, but the consensus in the industry right now is this: 50 words from an article (magazine or journal) and 250 words from a book or a book-length source (such as a screenplay) are okay without permission. Anything in excess of that needs to be reworked or requires permission. Keep those numbers in the back of your head as *guidelines*.

You should acknowledge sources whether you're quoting two words or 250 words. You should always acknowledge and credit someone else who you are quoting directly, and there are two ways to do that: in the text or as an endnote. Most of us are writing non-academic, conversational type books where endnotes are unnecessary.

Text references are as simple as putting the material into the flow of the sentence. If someone was quoting my editing book within their book, they could say something like this: "As Jodi Brandon wrote in *Become a Book Editor*, 'quoted material.'" You make it part of the sentence. It doesn't take away from the sentence but rather flows right in.

Having said that, legally speaking, acknowledgment may or may not be enough. Some copyright holders don't care about being credited in your book. They want to be paid. And the reason they want money is because they get to decide how much it's going to cost you to use their material. Let's say you want to use a 500-word section from a 50,000-word book. It's a small percentage, but it's enough that most publishers would require you to obtain permission or cut the material. Sometimes quotations lend themselves to being reduced while still making the point you want to make.

Other times it's not so easy. Sometimes you either need the whole thing, or you need nothing. If you decide you need the quote or excerpt, you need to obtain permission. Check the original source for the copyright holder, which you find on the copyright page of the book. If the book is traditionally published, write to the copyright holder in care of the publisher. If the source is a magazine/journal article, you'd contact the publication. For a blog post, the blog/site owner.

Many publishers have a section on their website for permissions requests. If they don't, send an email or letter to request permission. Include the following information:

- The exact excerpt you want to use,
- Your book title,
- Your print run (how many copies you're printing; if you're self-publishing you'll simply note that),
- Your publisher,
- Book price (tentative is OK),
- Book format(s),
- Book publication date,
- Publication details (e.g., word count), and
- Your contact information.

Individual publishers may require different/additional information; these are the standard elements. Be aware that this process can take several weeks. When you receive a response, it will include the fee if there is one as well as any other requirements, such as a specific credit line.

Organizing Your Research

You may think about going "old school" (AKA pen and paper, or notebooks). I love a new notebook as much as the next person, but I don't recommend that in this case. Remember this is probably more information than you've ever had to keep track of, organize, or maybe even had at your fingertips. It can become unwieldy fairly quickly. That said, if paper is what works for you, get some file folders and organize that way, but I recommend a digital tool like Evernote, Google Docs, Trello, or Asana. I organized this book in Trello, with sections of text in Google Drive. This system enabled me to move sections around within chapters until I had the order decided, capture screenshots of research to read, and more. I can easily imagine myself doing it that way again if I write another book.

The most important thing is that you have *a* system. You know how you work. Use what will work in the way your mind will be able to easily (and quickly) find what you need. Use something that you already have at your fingertips that you're already using, maybe for some other aspect of your business. (That's why I used Trello.) This isn't the time to try to learn a new system.

I organize my research by chapter once I have a rough table of contents from my brain dump. I don't mean Chapter 1, Chapter 2, and so forth; I mean by subject. For this book, I had a card in Trello for prewriting, one for fears, and one for editing, for example. When it was time to work on that chapter, everything I needed was right at my fingertips: interview notes, my own thoughts/notes, research notes, articles.

If you are scheduling interviews as part of your research, think about the time that will take. Do you want to schedule and complete interviews for a two-week block and try to get them done in that two-week block, and then use the next four weeks to do the rest of your research (reading, listening to podcasts, and taking notes)?

For book projects, I allow four weeks to research and spend two hours researching per weekday (one hour in the morning, and one hour after lunch). Any other time I come across something relevant to my book topic (outside of those dedicated research time blocks), I bookmark it until my next research session. I assign myself a general area to research (from the outline I created from my brain dumps) for each session. That process works well for me but may or may not work for you. Some of my clients prefer to block off one morning a week or two full days at the beginning of the process. Typically, this research process boils down to trial and error. Because most of us have not been in the classroom in many years, we're not in "student mode" where research and note-taking are second nature. Don't just block off two or three or six weeks on your calendar for "book research," though. You need to be strategic and deliberate.

Book Map

A book map is a fancy publishing term for the elements that a book includes and the order those elements appear. In the book publishing world, we break it down into three overall sections:

- Front matter,
- Body, and
- Back matter.

When you're self-publishing, for the most part you decide which elements you are going to include in your book. (I say "for the most part," because everyone needs, say a copyright page.) As the author, make sure your book designer is aware of the standard order of matter for books so that nothing in your book is out of place.

In March 2017, the Independent Book Publishers Association published an "industry standards checklist," to the joy of those of us in the book publishing world who work with self-publishing author-entrepreneurs. According to the IBPA website: "The purpose of the checklist is to give independent publishers an at-a-glance gauge of the professional presentation of any book in order to help level the playing field between indie publishers and large-scale conglomerates." The biggest concern I hear from author-entrepreneurs is that they want their self-published book to "look" like a traditionally published book. Following these guidelines is the best way to ensure that happens, and many of them are related to your book map. To decide which elements to include in your book, look at books similar to yours. Do most of them have, for example, a glossary or an appendix? If they do, you'll likely want to include one too. I advise clients to look at the reviews similar books have received for clues as to what readers like/don't like about those books. Sometimes those comments guide authors in creating their own book structure.

Front Matter

Copyright Page

You've likely seen various copyright pages. While they're each a bit different, they contain many of the same elements. Valid copyright declaration contains three parts:

1. The word *copyright* or the copyright symbol,
2. The year of creation/publication, and
3. The name of the copyright owner.

In addition to the copyright declaration, the copyright page also includes a reservation of rights (you've seen this in various forms; it starts "All rights reserved") and the publisher name and contact information. If you have a PO box, list that address. If you don't, put your city and state, and include a website address or email. You can credit here your editor, your designer, your illustrator, and anyone else who worked on the book, though this is not obligatory. You'll also include the book's ISBN (more on that later), Library of Congress control number (if you have one), and printing information (1st printing, 2nd printing, whatever is applicable, along with the country of printing). If you have a disclaimer, whether it be legal, medical, or other/general, it goes on the copyright page as well.

Table of Contents

The table of contents is the demarcation line for your book. Anything before that table of contents is not listed on the table of contents and does not have a numeric page number. Anything after the table of contents gets listed on the table of contents and has a numeric page number.

Foreword

The foreword is sort of like an introduction to or explanation of the book—and here's the key—*written by someone else.* Not all books have (or need) a foreword. If you do want a foreword for your book, ask someone who has some credibility and visibility within your industry to write it. This doesn't have to be someone famous, like a celebrity, but this person should have name recognition in your industry. If it's a name that your readers recognize, then right off the bat, even if they don't know you personally or know of you personally, this person that they do know is vouching for you.

Allow time in your schedule because whoever you approach will need to read the book, then craft the foreword. You might need to follow up a couple of times with them.

Preface and Introduction

The terms *preface* and *introduction* are often confused and sometimes used interchangeably. These are two different elements of a book, and they serve different purposes. The easiest way to remember the difference, according to my clients, is this: A preface describes how the book came to be—the purpose of the book. The introduction sets the stage for the reader and tells them what the book is about. The preface is how, the intro is what.

> *Don't Forget Your Call to Action*
>
> One of the great things about ebooks is that you can have a call to action page before readers even get to your content. Include a sales letter or ad to gather email addresses for your list at both the beginning and the end of your book. Here's a quick and easy way to

set up the page: a headline, a short paragraph (three or four sentences) describing whatever your opt-in is, a bulleted list of its benefits, and a call to action (Go to www.WebAddress.com to get your free opt-in [tell what it is: worksheet, checklist, etc.].)

Body

The body of the book is where your writing comes in: the chapters, anything within those chapters (graphics, images, captions for those images), and parts/sections if you have them. The body is self-explanatory.

Back Matter

I liken back matter to "extras": appendixes, resources, bibliographies, glossaries, samples (forms, swipe copy, etc.). You won't necessarily include all of these elements, but readers love anything they see as extra. If you can think of something that fits with your book, include it. This book has a glossary because there are terms—like book map—that you wouldn't know if you don't work in book publishing.

If you have an index (as nonfiction books typically do), it's also part of the backmatter.

About the Author: Front or Back?

This page establishes your credibility. It tells readers why you're worth listening to. As a reader, I prefer this in the back of the book, where traditional publishers put it, but I'm seeing more and more authors put it in the front matter with the dedication and acknowledgments. (Acknowledgments are being placed at the back of the book more and more often, too.

Perhaps by the third edition of *Write.Publish.Market.* this will be standard placement.)

Action Steps

Prewriting sets the stage for a smooth writing process. Taking time for this step to develop a solid outline, research plan, and book map is critical to the success of your book.

- Brain dump to determine your book contents.
- Choose a trim size for your book so you have a rough word count goal.
- Determine how much research you need to conduct and create a research plan of action.
- Seek permission for anything you want to quote that doesn't fall within "fair use" guidelines.
- Decide whether you want a foreword so you can approach that person with plenty of time before publication.

Chapter 4

First Draft and Revising

Let's get your book written! Are you ready? I know you're busy. After all, you're running a business. Lack of time is probably one of the reasons, if not *the* reason, you haven't written a book already.

Writing Schedule and Calendar

You know what a book is doing for other entrepreneurs. You can see how their books are serving their businesses: helping them build their platform and increase their credibility. Their books are doing all the things identified in Chapter 1 that you want to have happen for you (and your business). But how do you do it? You make the time. You are simply not going to *find* the time to write a book; your plate is already full. You have a family, you have your business, you have volunteer and church commitments, you have extended family obligations, and you have hobbies and other activities that you don't want to cut out of your life (think barre class, book club, weekly coffee with your local biz bestie).

No matter how much you may want to, you're simply not going to *find* the time. You have to *make* that time. This process is so individual and will look different for each of us. Think about where you can make time for the short term, whether that's cutting out a volunteer commitment or cutting out an extra hour of sleep. Remember that this is just for a short period of time, not forever.

> It's hard to make the time to write when it's not a direct income-producing activity.
> — Carrie Wilkerson

Most people can write about a thousand words in a writing session before they need to take a real break. The key is to allow enough time in a writing session to build writing rhythm. Too little time, and you might think, *Why bother?* Too much time, though, feels intimidating and overwhelming to even professional writers, let alone author-entrepreneurs who aren't used to producing a lot of words at a time (or maybe even writing regularly).

If we assume that you can write one thousand words per writing session, and you're planning one writing session per day, you'll need 50 writing days for a 50,000-word draft. Obviously, this is fluid because, as I mentioned previously, you're not targeting an absolute word count. (You'll have an idea, though, based on the research you do on competing titles, which will give you an idea of what's already published in your genre and if there are patterns as far as page count, topics, and more.)

Serious writers write, inspired or not. Over time they discover that routine is a better friend than inspiration.

— Ralph Keyes

Some people don't write every day. Some people don't write 1,000 words; they write once a week but do a 5,000-word session. Consider what will work for you and your lifestyle, and set up your writing calendar accordingly. As you build this calendar, keep in mind commitments that are already scheduled, such as vacations, as well as holidays and non-negotiable family time.

What you *don't* want to do is back yourself into a corner where you have to have the book done by a certain time (maybe it's due to your editor, or maybe you're attending an event where you're able to sell books), and you haven't given yourself any wiggle room.

I find it helpful to print a blank monthly calendar and physically cross off days when I am not planning a writing session. That helps my mind see that "50 writing sessions" is not the same as "50 days." It feels silly, but it works for me.

Logistics: Fitting Writing into Your Real Life
Many people plan or attend a writing retreat, whether by themselves or with a partner or small group. Others check themselves into a hotel for two or three nights. This type of concentrated writing works well for some people, but most of us cannot write "on demand," so be realistic about what you will be able to get done. (This type of writing is different from your regular writing

sessions, which you train yourself to do.) A concentrated time frame might allow you to get started and make headway, but it likely won't be enough time to write an entire book. Of course, being free of distractions is appealing, but if the environment is one we rarely experience (time alone at a hotel? Sign me up!), we're more inclined to relax than work.

Perhaps you can carve out some time in your schedule by taking advantage of a college-aged neighbor looking to babysit for an hour each morning, or signing up for a meal preparation service, grocery delivery, or a house cleaner for a two-month period.

Find your best time of the day for writing and write. Don't let anything else interfere.
— Esther Freud

Another option is to batch blog posts (and/or any other content you regularly produce) and find guest posters for your blog *before* your book writing time is set to begin. Then you can use the time you already have set aside for content creation to work on your book.

Writing Routine

You have a schedule now, but what does it look like to actually sit down and do that writing? You need a writing routine. You need a way to signal to your body and your brain that it's time to write. For decades professional writers have touted the importance of a writing routine, among them Stephen King,

Tobias Wolff, and Anthony Trollope. In *Rest,* author Alex Soojung-Kim Pang notes that "routines can enhance creativity," though most people think the opposite is true.

Think about your best time of day for productivity. Are you a morning person? A night owl? Don't say, "I'll wake up one hour early three days per week to write" if you're a night owl. (You won't.) Maybe you're unlike me, and you're best right after lunch (when I want to take a nap). Try to write at about the same time and in the same conditions every time. Unless you're battling a creative block and you need a change of scenery, the more often you sit in the chair in your office, the more often your brain will signal to the rest of your body that "It's go time. Start typing."

Also, think about your most productive and inspiring environment looks like. Do you need background noise? Is too much quiet bad for you, or does background noise drive you bananas? When I write, I like classical/instrumental music (which I don't listen to at any other time). Figure out what works for you. Some people cannot write at home. Some people need to be away from their home environment, where we're all more prone to distractions. Some people don't. I am fine in my office if my office door is closed. If my office door is open, I am too distracted. If the door is shut, though, with the music on, my body knows it's time to write. It's important to train yourself, and the way you do that is through consistently manufacturing that environment in which you're most inspired and productive.

Consistent action produces consistent results.
— Christine Kane

A word of caution: Even if background noise works for you, make sure your routine includes turning off your phone and social media distractions. You don't need your phone vibrating or beeping; you don't need to hear notifications from Facebook or Slack on your computer. In fact, I recommend not even being connected to the internet while writing. If I come across something I need to look up that I missed during my research phase, I simply note it in the manuscript, highlight it so I can find it later, and keep writing. It's hard to get writing momentum; don't lose it once you've found it!

> Trying to edit while writing is like trying to chop down a tree while you're climbing it.
> — Justin McLachlan

If distractions are a problem for you, check out apps like Calmly Writer and Writebox. (While we're speaking of apps, I also like Keep Writing, which doesn't let you delete. This removes the temptation to revise as you write.)

Perfect Setup Syndrome

As you establish your writing routine, I caution you: Do not get caught up in what I and others call perfect setup syndrome. *"Oh, if I don't have the music on today, it's not going to work." "If I don't have my coffee here on the right side of the computer instead of the left side of the computer, there goes my creativity."* Do not allow yourself to get wrapped up in trying to create the perfect conditions and the perfect situation because, honestly, it's more important to just write. Whatever your routine will be, create the routine and do it.

If you wait for inspiration to write, you're not a writer, you're a waiter.
— Dan Poynter

Last year a client told me on one of our book coaching calls, "As soon as my new desk chair comes, I'll have the perfect writing area in my office and can get started." Another client recently said, "After I land one more dream client, I'll be able to pay for childcare for two hours each afternoon and that time will be for writing my book." These are excuses *not* to write. You don't need the perfect space, the perfect time of day, or more time. Remember: You have to *make* time, not *find* time. Don't let these things hold you back.

Practice Makes Perfect

Do you write on a regular basis? You must practice writing to write a book. Even if you blog a couple of times a week, a few thousand words at a time, you're producing 6,000 or so words a week. A book is tens of thousands of words—a lot more words than you're used to writing. The way to train yourself to do that is to practice, and the way you practice is to write every day. You can write anything at all. I love the website 750words.com. You type directly into the "document" on the site, and it tells you when you've reached 750 words. You also receive stats from each session, like total time, total writing time, and total word count produced. There are also many websites and books with writing prompts if that's more your style.

Professional writing advice notes that building a writing habit is part of perfecting your craft. You're try-

---

ing to build a habit to make writing this book easier, not perfect a writing craft so professional writing life is easier. Writing every day is a piece of writing advice that works for everyone, professionals and amateurs alike. (My clients would tell you I'm the first to tell you to ignore some of the writing advice out there, but not this time.)

Writing is a muscle that gets stronger with use.
— Abbi Glines

Tracking Your Progress

If you're unsure of just how to establish a strong routine, experiment a bit, and track the writing sessions. Keep track, whether in a notebook or a Google doc, the time spent writing, the word count, the setting, your feelings (Were you feeling inspired? Did the writing come easy? Was it hard to get started?), and anything else that might have affected the writing session. An entry might look like this:

> 4/1/19
> 10 a.m.
> 25 min
> 680 words
> home office
> hard to get started but easy after ~ 10 min in
> neighbor mowing lawn right outside office

This record will help you see patterns. Maybe you'll find that there's too much noise in your neighborhood to write on weekday afternoons in the summer. (I live in a wonderful development full of kids who play outside, ride their bikes, and play basketball across the street, which is fun—except when I'm trying to write, since mostly quiet is what works for me.) Maybe you'll find that Starbucks is not a great spot for you but that the local mom-and-pop coffee house is. Maybe you'll find that you're just too tired mentally after a full day of work to use your brain for writing. Track it for a couple of weeks (writing every day) and see what helps you be most productive.

Use Your Voice

If you hate the thought of sitting at a computer for an extra hour each day, dictate your book to draft your manuscript. Download a voice-recording app or software onto your smartphone and dictate the first draft.

Dictate the book, and have it transcribed. (Among many popular transcription apps is Rev.com, which costs $1 per minute as of this writing.) Then instead of staring at a blank piece of paper (if you're old school) or a blank computer screen, you have a draft to work with. You might have more work to do in the self-editing and revising stages, but if that's what it takes for you to get a draft finished, then, by all means, speak away.

Write the Introduction Last

Most people want to start writing by writing the introduction. You're ready to write, and you figure the introduction is the beginning of the book, so that's what you should write first. Think back to the difference between an outline and a brain dump. Whereas the outline is formal, structured, and rigid, the brain dump is free-flowing and fluid. It changes during the writing process. Think of the introduction in a similar vein. If you write the introduction first, based on what you *think* the book is going to be (*My book is about this. First, I talk about this, and then I move on to this, and then I move on to that,*) in the back of your mind, you are trying to make your book "fit" that introduction, and that might not be the right structure for your book.

Let your book develop organically and take on a life of its own. Unfortunately, sometimes that means moving text/ sections around and making changes. You might get the entire manuscript written and then when you read it, think, *Chapter 7 really needs to come between chapters 2 and 3, because if I don't move that there, then it doesn't make sense when I talk about X, Y, Z in Chapter 4.* Or, *Now that I'm re-reading Chapter 5, I think I should take the second half of that chapter and move it to the beginning of Chapter 9. It fits better there.*

If you already have your introduction written, it can be harder (psychologically) for you to make the changes, even though you know you should.

Another bonus of writing the introduction last is that it essentially writes itself. Think about it: The book is written. There's no "This is what I'm going to talk about first. This is what I'm going to talk about next." The text is already there, fleshed out. Writing the beginning at the end goes against a lot of our natural tendencies (because we want to start at the beginning), but I encourage you to give this method a try.

So where *should* you start? Take a look at your brain dump, pick a topic for which you have lots of notes taken (then you won't have any reason to say, "I don't know what to write," because you have all this research to pull from), start there, and gain some momentum.

Best-selling author Michael Hyatt agrees that writing sequentially is not necessary. Instead, in an interview with Chandler Bolt's Self-Publishing Summit, Hyatt says to start with a section that you think will be easy to write. This will help you build confidence as well as momentum.

Revising: Not a "One and Done" Process

Your goal when revising is to improve your manuscript. Clarify where needed. Remove tangents and extraneous text. Reorganize sections as needed. You may need to do a lot of revision, or you may need to do little. It depends on your writing style, how much prewriting you did, and your natural writing ability.

The number of revision rounds is up to you when you're self-publishing. There is no "right" number (though I can tell you with confidence that it's more than one). No one can tell you your manuscript is "ready" to be published (though your editor will likely try!). Ideally, you are finding less and less to change with each round of revision. (The truth is you can always improve a manuscript. But if you aim for perfection, you'll never publish your book because you won't deem it "ready.")

Did you notice I referred to "rounds of revision"? That's because, ideally, you'll be revising at one time, not throughout the writing process. If you finish a draft and then review it as a whole work, you'll have an easier time seeing issues that you need to address.

Action Steps

Writing a complete manuscript is a considerable undertaking. Breaking the process into manageable steps helps you stay on track and avoid overwhelm.

- Create a writing schedule with a target completion date for your first draft.
- Decide what your most productive writing session looks like and create a writing routine around it.
- After a break from the manuscript, revise.

PART II: PUBLISH

Chapter 5
Manuscript Preparation

Your work is far from over once your first draft is finished. The first step after you've taken a break (you *did* celebrate finishing your draft and take a break from looking at this document, didn't you?) is to prepare your manuscript for publication.

Self-Editing

One of the biggest "cons" of self-publishing, according to many self-published authors (including many of my author-entrepreneur clients), is that you have to shell out some money before your book is published. Books that are not professionally edited contain errors, sloppy writing, and more, so professional editing is a smart investment to make when self-publishing.

Chapter 6 discusses editing in greater depth. For now, let me say this: Before you work with a professional editor, you should self-edit your book. I know, I know: You aren't an expert in grammar or transitions between paragraphs or concise writing. You'll be amazed at what you can find on your own, though, and clean up.

The "cleaner" your manuscript is when it goes to an editor (meaning the fewer outright errors it has), the less work it needs. The less work it needs, the less time the editor will require. The less time it takes, the less editing will cost you. This is true whether your editor bills by the hour, by the page, or by the word.

What does it mean to self-edit your manuscript? Here are some first steps:

First and most importantly: Step back. Give yourself as much time as possible away from the manuscript as you can. That may be a couple of days; it may be a couple of weeks. Any time you can take so that, when you open the document again, it's with a fresh set of eyes will greatly benefit your work. You'll be amazed when you see typos jumping out at you, words you left out, and sentences that aren't quite clear—things you can't believe you missed the other 50 times you read that sentence. Trust me: This happens to every person who has ever written a book—and leads me right into the next tip.

Self-edit in stages. Just like an editor won't catch everything the first time through, neither will you. Once you've taken some time away, read your manuscript once in entirety for the big picture (macro level), then read again for details (micro level). Reading for the big picture allows you to ensure the manuscript flows as a whole unit. You may recognize sections that need to be rewritten to help the reader transition to the next topic or section, or this step may show you a different way to structure the chapters or material within a chapter. You'll have caught some of these when revising, but, again, it's amazing what will reveal itself to you after a bit of time away from the manuscript. When reading on the micro level, be on the hunt for typos and grammatical errors. These errors may seem small and insignificant, but eliminating them shows that you care about your work down to the smallest detail. It lends a sense of professionalism and seriousness to you and your work. (Think about how you feel as a reader when you see a typo or mistake.) With each pass of the manuscript, you should find fewer and fewer errors.

Also read the manuscript aloud, so you *hear* the mistakes that your eyes, after reading the same sentence multiple times while writing and rewriting, miss. Your eyes often read the text as your brain intended—which may or may not be what you've actually written. Reading aloud provides another way to ensure your manuscript is ready for the next stage of the publishing process. I also suggest reading paragraphs backward, starting with the last sentence, to catch any lingering errors. This might feel silly at first, but that silliness goes away when you realize how many errors you find (and correct).

Your manuscript is now improved based on these practices. To improve it even further, and if you really want to impress an editor, here are a few specific, micro-level tips:

- Refresh your memory of some basic grammar "rules": who vs. whom, that vs. which, between vs. among. Your editor will surely catch these, but wouldn't you rather they be focused on clarity and tone, rather than nitty-gritty errors?
- Almost always delete *really* and *very*. They're almost always unnecessary because they rarely add anything of substance to your work.
- Avoid absolutes where possible (*always, never*). There are exceptions to just about every statement you could make. Add a qualifier if you aren't using specific numbers (usually, almost always—like I did

in the previous bullet point when talking about *really* and *very*).

- Eliminate passive voice. Which sentence reads more smoothly?

    Julie confirmed the dinner reservation.

    The dinner reservation was confirmed by Julie.

    The second sentence sounds clunky. Your audience wants to be where the action is!

- Use—but do not rely on—spellcheck. It won't catch homonyms (e.g., to vs. too vs. two) or instances where you've used the wrong word, but that word is an actual word (e.g., *rather that* when you meant *rather than*).

- Learn which dash to use when: hyphens, en-dashes (with series of numbers), and em-dashes (used, often in pairs, with text that's an aside).

- Brush up on apostrophe usage. Know the difference between plurals and possessives.

- Treat numbers consistently. Pick a style and stick with it. Some publishers spell out numbers up to ninety-nine. Others spell out only one through nine. As long as you're consistent throughout the work, you can choose any style you want. (Let your editor know what you've decided.)

- Watch out for over-capitalization. Capitalizing terms to give them a sense of importance is something I see all the time (and something that drives me, and most editors, bonkers). It's also a dead giveaway that you didn't have your book edited.

- Don't skip headings! You would be shocked at how

many books have errors in chapter titles and headings because authors (and sometimes editors, too) skip over these, assuming they are correct.

- Following these self-editing tips won't ensure that your manuscript is error-free, but it will produce a cleaner manuscript that requires less work and less time from an editor. That means you'll be on the road to publication even sooner (and with more money in your pocket).

Beta Feedback

You want to get your manuscript, as far as its actual content, as close to perfect as you can before publication because later it's more time-consuming and sometimes more expensive to make changes and correct errors. Your goal is to send the strongest manuscript you can to the editor and then the designer. The way to do that is to get feedback using beta readers, which are people who read an unfinished version of the manuscript and provide feedback to help you improve it. Beta readers will point out anything that doesn't make sense: a concept that isn't clear/fleshed out, a term that needs to be defined better (or sooner), a story that does not resonate, and more. All of these manuscript notes will help you strengthen the manuscript.

How do you know what feedback to incorporate and what not to? Let's say you have five beta readers for your manuscript. If one or two people mention that one section of your manuscript is unclear, then maybe they just don't understand your subject area the way the other betas do. If four out of five are not getting what you're saying, though, you should probably take a look at that section and see how you can improve it.

> Beta feedback isn't about you. It's about your book.
> — Amanda Shofner

Beta readers should provide both positive and negative feedback. This is why I suggest that you reach beyond your network of people to find them. Your network can surely offer suggestions for beta readers, and you can certainly have your network of people read the manuscript, but be aware that the feedback you get will mainly be positive. No one wants to criticize their friends or their colleagues, so often the feedback is along the lines of "I loved it!" and "This is so good"—nice to hear, to be sure, but not helpful to strengthen your manuscript. The purpose of the beta reading stage is to improve your manuscript, not stroke your ego. If you're only getting positive feedback, that purpose is not being fulfilled.

Finding Beta Readers

So where do you find betas if you're not using your network directly? First, if you Google "beta reader," you will come up with lots of people as well as lots of beta reading services that have people in certain topic areas and genres. Another great resource is Goodreads, which has a beta forum. (I've had a lot of success there, as have quite a few of my clients.) You can also post in Facebook groups you belong to or tweet about what you're looking for. If you have a client or two who you think can and will provide constructive feedback, they are great people to ask because of their familiarity with you/your process.

Note: Do *not* pay for beta reading. Some beta readers charge authors to read your manuscript. Skip them!

Logistics: Numbers and Process

How many people are you looking for? "The more, the merrier" might seem like a good motto here, but it can backfire. The more opinions you enlist, the more you could get—leaving you even more confused than when you started. If you can find five to eight people, that's a good number for the types of books author-entrepreneurs write.

Once you've identified your beta readers, then what? Ask the people you've selected to gauge their interest, and include in that communication your time line. Maybe someone seems like a perfect beta reader but will be on vacation when your manuscript will be ready for feedback. Or maybe they'll be on maternity leave at the time you'll need the feedback returned. Start with your wish list of betas, and fill in as needed based on scheduling.

Give betas at least two weeks if your production schedule allows, so they don't feel rushed. And let them know in advance when to expect the manuscript (and when their feedback will be due). Pro tip: Don't give them *too* much time with the manuscript or it will become an item on their to-do list that gets put off (*I have plenty of time, so no need to start that today.*) and then, possibly, rushed at the end. In that scenario, you don't get the most helpful feedback.

You can ask beta readers to provide feedback in one of two ways: They can write a reader's report—a few paragraphs of what they liked, what they thought needed improvement, and so forth. You could also set up a survey in a free survey tool like Typeform where you ask questions, such as:

- Was the transition between Chapter 3 and Chapter 4 smooth?

- Were there areas of the manuscript that needed clarification? If so, please explain.
- Were there any terms that needed to be defined? If yes, please list.
- Did the case study of Miranda make sense even though its conclusion is still up in the air?

If you use a survey, you're getting feedback but in a guided way. Which method you use is a matter of preference. The survey method is more foolproof, in my experience, and is the easiest way for beta readers to understand what you're looking for from them.

Beta Readers vs. Editors

Beta readers do not take the place of editors (no matter what your fiction-writing independent author friends tell you!). Some of what beta readers will point out *could* be similar to what an editor finds on his or her initial read, as both are looking at your manuscript with a fresh eye and pointing out areas in your manuscript that might require tweaking. The key difference is that beta readers don't have any training and probably don't have the experience that an editor has to take it one step further. In an editor, you want someone who not only is going to point out where a manuscript needs improvement, but also offer a solution to strengthen your manuscript.

Solutions are not a beta reader's responsibility. Don't get me wrong: If you find a great beta reader with years of experience, particularly in your genre, they may offer a solution, but that is definitely the exception, not the rule—and if they do, they are going above and beyond. The caution for you as an author is this: The beta feedback process is not of the same as professional editing, so please don't think you can skip right over hiring an editor because you enlisted beta readers. They serve different functions.

When to Obtain Beta Feedback

Different schools of thought exist on when to obtain beta feedback. As a copy editor, I prefer as complete a manuscript as possible, so I encourage clients to obtain and incorporate beta feedback after they revise and self-edit, but before the manuscript lands on my desk.

Testimonials

When you receive positive feedback from beta readers, spin it into a testimonial. Ask beta readers if you can use their compliments as a testimonial. (You also want them to write a review after your book is released; we'll talk about that in Chapter 11.) Testimonials fall into the category of "once you have one, it's easy to get more."

You need testimonials to use to market your book. You can even use a short, powerful testimonial on your front cover. You can use them on the back cover. You can use them on your website and in your promotional material. There's no such thing as too much good feedback or too many testimonials.

You'll be able to get more as your book reaches more people, but using early feedback for your initial testimonials helps you start strong.

Pricing

Pricing your book can be tricky. You don't want to price too low and have people think there's no value within those pages. You don't want to overprice, either, or you'll lose valuable readers. Think about who your audience is, what their knowledge level is, and how other books in your genre and bookstore category are priced. The price of your book should not be based solely on the size (trim size/number of pages) and format (paperback/hardcover/ebook) of your book. Your readers are paying for content, not the physical properties of the book. Most paperback books in the business, resource, and personal development genres and the 100- to 200-page range are priced between $8.99 and $14.99.

KDP (Amazon's publishing arm) and IngramSpark both have royalty calculators on their sites for author-entrepreneurs to use. These allow you to enter your book specs (price, page count, color vs. black and white interior, for example) and see what your royalties would be based on that information. If you're a planner of any kind, you'll have fun playing around with these.

Obtaining an ISBN

ISBN stands for International Standard Book Number. It's the 13-digit number on the copyright page of a book and above the bar code on the back cover of a print book. Publishers and booksellers use the ISBN for various reasons, none of which you need to worry about as an author-entrepreneur. What you *do* need to know is this: When you apply for an ISBN, you'll be listed as the publisher of record for your book. If you publish through Amazon, they can assign you an ISBN for free. You'll read much more about this in Chapter 9. For now, though, here's the bottom line: You want to be the publisher of record for your book, and that means purchasing your own ISBN.

In the United States, ISBNs must be purchased from a

company called Bowker (myidentifiers.com). I have no idea why, but they have a monopoly on selling barcodes and ISBNs in the United States. The process is simple and only takes a few minutes. You will have the option of purchasing one, 10, 100, or 1,000 ISBNs. If you purchase one, as of May 2019, the cost is $125. If you purchase 10, it's $295. Every format of your book requires a different ISBN (hardcover, paperback, large-print, etc.), so it might make financial sense for you to purchase a block of ISBNs. You don't need to use them all at the time of purchase. Bowker will assign them to you, and you can hang on to them until you have another format of this book (or another book).

If you're not in the United States, know that there is one place to purchase ISBNs in each country. (It varies by country.) Another that I'm familiar with is Canada: If you're publishing in Canada and you register your book with the government, you can get an ISBN free.

Your designer will need the ISBN for your back cover, so purchase this, for example, while your manuscript is with your editor or during the break between revision and self-editing. You can purchase any time after your title and subtitle are final. As I mentioned, it only takes a few minutes.

ISBNs for Ebooks: Pros and Cons

Pros
- Your book will be easier to find.
- Your book could have more distribution channels.
- ISBNs lend an air of professionalism and credibility.

Cons
- ISBNs cost money.
- The book publishing industry hasn't found a direct correlation between an ISBN and ebook sales.

Filing Copyright

What is copyright? Essentially, copyright is protection for your intellectual property—in this case, your words. As soon as a work is fixed in a tangible form, copyright belongs to the creator. Your work is copyrighted as soon as it's written (that is, in fixed form), whether that be on a computer screen or a napkin. If you file copyright formally, you have an extra layer of protection if your work is plagiarized. My understanding of the law (remember here that I am not a lawyer) is that authors cannot file copyright infringement suits unless they've registered their work with the U.S. Copyright Office.

Is the $35 it costs to file with the U.S. Copyright Office worth it? That's up to you. (For me, *yes*.) If you decide to register, simply go to www.copyright.gov, pay the fee, and upload an electronic version of your book before publication. The process is straightforward and simple.

Action Steps

Don't make the mistake of thinking your work is done when your manuscript is finished. You still have quite a bit to do to ready your book for publication.

- Self-edit your manuscript so that it's as clean as possible before a professional editor sees it.
- Choose beta readers and submit the manuscript for feedback.
- Set your price for each format of your book (paperback, ebook, audiobook, etc.).
- Obtain an ISBN.

Chapter 6
Editing: Get Your Writing Right

When you publish traditionally, the publishing house will assign a production editor to your book. When you self-publish, it's up to you to find and pay for an editor if you want to have your book edited before publication. (Hint: You do.) You're the boss when self-publishing, so of course you don't *have* to have your book edited. (But really, you do.) I worked solely as a book editor for 15 years and still do one-on-one editing work, so I'm clearly an advocate for professional editing. My reason is simple: You're an expert in your industry; an editor is an expert in theirs. Editors make your text read smoother, and your book will be without silly proofreading errors that can hurt your credibility. Most people think of copy editors when they think of editors, but there's more to editing than that.

> Everyone needs an editor.
> — Tim Foote

What Is Editing?
Some people call editors the bridge between an author and an audience. Merriam-Webster.com defines *editing* as "to prepare

something written, to be published or used: to make changes, correct mistakes, etc. in (something written)."

You know from this book's Introduction that the writing process has five stages. There are multiple stages of editing as well. Once your manuscript is written, you might wonder what comes next. Before you look into hiring an editor, let's review the various types of editing and how you know what you need.

Developmental Editing

You will reach a point in your writing when you have spilled everything out onto your computer screen, but then wonder how to organize it all. A developmental editor can help make sense of your writing. They will be able to guide you in forming chapters, flow, pace, tone, and the overall structure of your book. Think of developmental editing, which is sometimes called structural editing, as looking at the big picture of your manuscript. Depending on your natural writing and organizational abilities, you may or may not require a developmental edit.

Keep in mind that some developmental editors prefer to work on projects as they're being written, rather than after they're drafted.

Copy Editing

Copy editing is the type of editing most people think of when they hear the word *editor*. It is all about the details at the copy editing stage. You've been reading and re-reading your manuscript, but it comes time for a copy editor to step in. Let the editor read it with a fresh set of eyes. They will make sure details are consistent throughout the book (e.g., voice, tense, even spelling), correct grammar and mechanics issues, and ensure clarity throughout your manuscript. If your message is lost in your writing, then it doesn't matter, frankly, if you've followed grammar rules.

Proofreading

A proofreader will give the manuscript one last look; they will find stray typos or notice the formatting is just a bit off, ensuring that everything is just right for publication. Specifically, they'll be performing tasks that include matching page numbers against the contents, checking headers, looking for even spacing before and after bulleted lists, and ensuring that bibliography entries are in alphabetical order. Proofreading is done after a book is formatted.

All manuscripts can benefit from a copy edit and a proofread, but it can be expensive. Expect to spend a few hundred dollars minimum (up to upward of a thousand dollars) on copy editing; the editor's fee depends on how much work is required on your manuscript, as discussed in Chapter 5. For this reason, some self-publishing authors skip copy editing. At the bare minimum, hire a professional proofreader. The expense will be less, but you can rest easier knowing that you had a professional look at the typeset book before it was printed/uploaded. Better for the proofreader to find typos than your readers! If you have any concerns about the organization, structure, or tone of your book (to name just a few), though, know that a proofread alone will not address them.

Some editors offer all three services; others specialize in one or two types/levels. I recommend getting multiple sets of eyes on your book manuscript rather than using the same editor for every stage. (Just as your brain starts to read what it thinks you wrote, your editor will look at your material so much that *their* brains will eventually start to do the same.) Good editors will be up-front about where your manuscript is, which service(s) your book needs, and they can help you.

> A very good editor is almost a collaborator.
> — Ken Follett

Questions to Ask Potential Editors

A good working relationship between author and editor is essential, or your manuscript will suffer. An editor is part of your book team, and a good editor wants to make a manuscript better and ready it for publication. Talk with potential editors on the phone or via Zoom if you can; don't rely solely on email communication before hiring your editor. You need to know if your personalities are a good fit, as you will be working closely with the editor on your manuscript. Think about how much hard work you have put into your writing; you want to make sure your editor is someone with whom you can entrust your manuscript and are comfortable.

Note that no professional editor can guarantee either a perfect, error-free manuscript or measurable success on publication (such as X number of books sold or best-seller status).

Before hiring an editor or signing a contract, ask the following questions:

What Does the Process Look Like?

Generally, editors of nonfiction books want a completed manuscript before they'll start editing. The process will vary, as all editors have their own working style, but generally, an editor will review the manuscript and return it to you with queries and comments, using Microsoft Word's "Track Changes" feature. The editor may do a second (or even a third) pass on the manuscript if there are a lot of queries or changes to be made; you'll negotiate that before editing begins.

Do You Have References I Can Speak With?

If an editor won't share any names, this is a major red flag. You want to work with someone who has past clients singing their praises! Most editors' websites have a testimonials or praise page, too.

What is Your Editing Background?

Because the United States does not have a formal certification program for book editing, anyone can set up shop and sell their services as a book editor. It's important, then, that you do your homework. Does the editor have a website? Does the editor have references or a list of books they've worked on? (Don't rely just on that, as often editors aren't allowed to disclose book titles. I have a few *New York Times* best-sellers on my list, but they are not listed on my website due to confidentiality.) What is the editor's experience? How long has the editor been practicing their craft? Trust your gut. You are looking for a professional editor, not someone who "was good at English" in school. (That said, I bet your editor did, in fact, get good English grades!) Editing is about so much more than understanding the rules and nuances of the English language.

How Much Will it Cost?

This depends on several factors, among them the type or types of editing you need (and can afford), how clean the manuscript is, and whether it is a rush project. For a typical nonfiction book (and I emphasize the word *range* here, because these books can be as few as 30,000 words up to 100,000 words and more; obviously your word count will factor in here in a major way), you can expect to pay anywhere from a few hundred dollars to a few thousand dollars for a copy edit. A developmental edit would cost more than that and is typically charged by the hour rather than by the page or word, and a proofread will cost the least.

What Makes You a Good Editor for My Manuscript?

Ask the editor what they see in the manuscript that makes for a good fit between you and them. Maybe your manuscript is about heart disease prevention, and the editor's father has heart disease; that would be a good subject matter fit, as the editor probably has more basic, everyday knowledge about heart disease than most people and can ask you more in-depth questions about areas you might want to expand upon to strengthen your book. Or maybe your book has a lot of issues with punctuation and your potential editor is a grammar specialist (even more so than other editors you speak with).

How Long Will Editing Take?

A good editor won't propose a schedule without looking at your manuscript (or at least part of it). Without seeing the text, they have no way to know how to clean the text, and thus no way to know how long editing will take. (If you want to reduce editing time, take a look at the self-editing tips in Chapter 5.) Also remember that an editor is running a business, too. Good editors are booked several weeks or even months in advance, so find someone as early as you can, pay a deposit (usually), and secure a spot on their calendar once you have a solid writing plan in place and an idea of when you'll be ready to submit your manuscript.

Have You Edited a Book Like Mine Before?

This may or may not be important to you. Some editors specialize in a certain genre of book (say, business books or cookbooks or memoirs); others are generalists. If your content is quite specific, it might benefit you to work with someone who's edited books similar to yours.

Are You Willing to Provide an Editing Sample?

You'll have to weigh whether this is a make-or-break issue for you. Many editors provide a sample edit; many don't. Some will provide a sample for a fee. Samples can be a wonderful tool for editors to show their value because, as an author-entrepreneur, you can see quickly the amount and types of errors your manuscript contains.

Where to Find Editors

Check local sources if budget is a real concern: teachers at local high schools or colleges who might be looking for extra income (particularly during the summer months), or members of writers' groups. You'll also find editors on sites like Elance and Fiverr. Remember, though, that you get what you pay for; these are usually not professional editors, so the quality of service won't be the same as a professional editor would provide.

> A good editor can be a writer's best friend.
> — Andrea Merrell

Word-of-mouth is likely the best way to find an editor. You can, of course, Google "book editor" but you'll spend hours wading through websites of editors to make a short list of people to contact. Ask for recommendations in Facebook groups, your mastermind, or in-person networking groups you belong to. Not only will you get names this way, but you can get an insider's perspective of what it's like to work with a particular editor; that's even better than a testimonial any day of the week.

The-EFA.org is the website of the Editorial Freelancers Association, to which many professional editors belong. EFA has a job board where authors can advertise a project for free, and the post is sent to the EFA membership to apply directly to you. Writer's Market offers a similar service for a fee.

Action Steps

A professional editor can improve your manuscript. Understand the value of the investment in this work.

- Know what kind(s) of editor your book needs.
- Ask potential editors the questions in this chapter to ensure you hire the right person for the job.

Chapter 7
Formatting Your Book Interior: It's Gotta Look Good!

Among the myriad reasons so many publishing professionals advocate self-publishing these days is because it's possible to publish a professional product. (Remember that standards checklist I mentioned previously?) Authors who are writing a draft in 10 days, not editing, purchasing a cover template from Amazon, and then publishing, give the rest of the industry a bad name—because some readers assume that's what all self-publishing authors are doing.

Just as I said in Chapter 6 about editors: Designers are experts at design, just as your expertise is in your industry. Do you have the time and inclination to learn how to properly (and aesthetically) design a book? If so, then go for it. If not, though, then hire someone. And by "someone," I mean someone who designs books, not someone who designs other products. Author-entrepreneurs, in particular, tend to do this, and their thinking makes sense: You likely have a team member who's a designer. They know your brand well (heck, they may have even developed it!) and you work well together.

For a book, though, I caution you to hire someone who

designs books specifically. Book design is an art form, even if your book is just text (meaning you have no images or graphics). Designing a book correctly and beautifully is not nearly as easy as designers make it look! The fact that we don't notice the design means the designer has done their job. The ultimate goal is readability, so really, book design is an invisible art.

Another consideration with regard to book design is whether or not you have the proper tools. Books should not be formatted in Microsoft Word. Adobe InDesign is the popular program of choice for designers, but it's expensive and probably not worth the cost if you're using it for a one-off project.

If you decide to handle formatting yourself, though—and I know many author-entrepreneurs do to save money, even when they know they cannot compete with what a professional can do—Joel Friedlander's site, the Book Designer (www.thebooksdesigner.com), is a great resource.

Questions to Ask Potential Designers

Your book designer is another member of your book team. As you did before hiring an editor, talk with potential designers on the phone or via Zoom if possible.

Before signing a contract with a designer, ask the following questions:

What Does the Design Process Look Like?

The process will depend on the designer, as all designers have their own working styles and processes. Generally, the designer will want to know your estimated word count, the trim size you're considering, and the general concept (text only, text plus photos, text plus charts, etc.). The designer will build a schedule that allows for review before the design is final.

Do You Have References I Can Speak With?

Most designers have books they've designed listed on their website. If their site doesn't allow you to "look inside," look up a couple of the books on Amazon, where you can. In addition to seeing their work, speak to a couple of authors they have worked with to get an idea of their communication style.

How Much Will it Cost?

This depends on several factors, among them the size of your book, whether or not you have straight text or text plus graphics of some kind, and whether they're designing the cover as well as the interior. You can expect to pay anywhere from a few hundred dollars to a couple of thousand dollars for interior book design.

How Long Will the Design Take?

Again, this depends on many factors, first and foremost of which is how complicated the design will be. Designers, like editors, are booked several weeks or even months in advance, so you want to find someone as early as you can, pay a deposit (usually), and secure a spot on their calendar.

Have You Designed a Book Like Mine Before?

This matters more if your book has, for example, many images or is a specialty book, such as a cookbook or craft how-to book. In these cases, it might benefit you to work with someone who's designed books similar to yours.

Where to Find Designers

You'll find designers on sites like Elance and Fiverr, just as you do editors. Again, remember that you get what you pay for. Word-of-mouth is a great resource for finding a designer.

Ask for recommendations in groups you belong to, whether online or in-person. Individual designers, as well as book design firms, such as the Book Designers, are available for book interiors.

Order of Matter

Remember the book map we discussed in Chapter 3? Here's where it comes into play. Your front matter and back matter should follow the standard order used in book publishing. Otherwise, it's a dead giveaway that your book was self-published. Your designer should know this order, but if they don't, or if you've decided to format the book yourself, keep this section handy. Remember that your book might not have all of these elements, and that's perfectly fine. (The body of the book is just that—no special notes on order needed.)

Front Matter
- Half-title page (optional),
- Title page,
- Copyright page,
- Dedication,
- Acknowledgments (can also be placed in back matter),
- Contents,
- Foreword,
- Preface, and
- Introduction.

Back Matter
- Appendixes,
- Notes,
- Glossary,
- Resources,

- Index, and
- About the Author.

Book Format Basics

The standard EPUB format is used by all the major booksellers except Amazon, which uses the MOBI format. Ingram distribution (more on that in Chapter 10) reaches all of the major booksellers, retail partners, and library partners; Amazon handles its own distribution. MOBI format is not limited to Kindle thanks to the Kindle app. Anyone with the app can read MOBI files on mobile devices, tablets (including iPads), and computers. Most ebook formatters create an EPUB and then modify it for MOBI. It's inexpensive to have this done for you and confusing to do it yourself, so I recommend hiring someone to handle the conversion formatting for you.

There are, of course, also PDFs, which you can sell directly from your website. To do that you'd need an automated payment system linked to your site, such as Gumroad. A couple of advantages to selling on your own site are that you can sometimes charge a higher price since you already have an ongoing relationship with most of your customers, and you're keeping even more money. That said, the more places you have your ebook and book available, the better chance you have of new customers finding you (AKA people who don't already know you).

Heading Hierarchy

Headings are signposts for readers. Brooke Warner of She Writes Press, at the 2019 Independent Book Publishers Association conference, likened subheads to buckets and said, "[T]hrow in everything you want to say about that topic, but don't let overflow from other subjects spill in." The heading hierarchy is important to you, as the author, as far as organizing your content. For readers, though, it's a visual way to move through the book.

Your book will likely have headings as well as various levels of subheadings. Right now you're in the Heading Hierarchy subsection of the Book Format Basics section, for example.

Use the styles in Word to style these correctly rather than manually making headings larger or using a different font. This way, your designer won't have any confusion about the hierarchy you intend. Set up the styles in your project so that formatting does not look wonky when you're ready to print or upload your book.

Trim Size

As mentioned previously, the two most common trim sizes for trade nonfiction books are 5x8 inches and 6x9 inches. What size are other books in your genre? If most are the same size, it makes sense to use that. Consider also your word count. You don't want an 80-page, 6x9 book priced at $10.99. Most people will think it's overpriced and move on to the next book that showed up in their search results.

What's the Investment?

The investment for book design depends on several factors, most notably your word count and whether or not your book has graphics of any kind. Formatting a photography book, for example, will cost much more than novel formatting. A business book with figures and tables throughout will cost more than a business book that is text only.

Expect to spend anywhere from a couple of hundred dollars to a couple of thousand dollars depending on the design complexity of your particular project and the designer's experience.

Action Steps

The design process is when your words become a book, rather than a manuscript. Not all design work is equal, so hiring someone with experience designing books is crucial.

- Ask the questions in this chapter to make sure you hire the right designer for your project.
- Give your designer the book map to ensure they know the order of matter for your book.

Chapter 8
First Impressions: Cover and Title

Title

You may have an idea of what your title will be when you start writing. That's okay. You may not. That's okay, too. You might have a revelation during the writing process when you write a sentence and think, *That's it. That's the title.* As you move closer to publication, though, you'll need the title and subtitle. You'll need them for your cover, to get your ISBN, and to get the book/ebook listed on Amazon and elsewhere, among myriad other reasons. The book cover may be the reader's first impression, but keep in mind that many times people won't see the cover but *will* see or read the title somewhere.

When brainstorming titles, consider the time-result formula, which readers are often drawn to. Sometimes this formula works for a great subtitle, too. The formula looks like this: X amount of time to achieve X results in a numeric format. Here are a few examples:

- 5 Steps to In-box Zero
- 10 Ways to Earn Amazon Bestseller Status
- 20 Recipes to Lose 15 Pounds in 2 Weeks

Write your book and then see how the title fits. You can

also get suggestions from friends, colleagues, and clients to test and validate ideas.

Remember that shorter is usually better for the title. Also think about how you can make it memorable in some way, such as using alliteration. Many author-entrepreneurs prefer a short title and a longer, keyword-rich subtitle. Often that's where you'll find the benefits of a book, for example—so perhaps a term or two that potential readers would be searching for on Google or Amazon.

You can play with various combinations of words/phrases by using a thesaurus as well as see what auto-populates in Google and Amazon search boxes when you type in your overall book topic. Many authors try to squeeze in every keyword they can. Be wary of doing this, as you can easily end up with quite a mouthful for a subtitle. Getting it right can take some finagling, so don't rush this exercise!

Here are a few titles/subtitles that strike the right balance of informative and succinct, with the words people might type into a search box to have these titles appear in a search underlined:

- *Playing Big: Practical <u>Wisdom</u> for Women Who Want to <u>Speak</u> Up, <u>Create</u>, and <u>Lead</u>*
- *Daring Greatly: How the <u>Courage</u> to Be <u>Vulnerable</u> <u>Transforms</u> the Way We <u>Live</u>, <u>Love</u>, <u>Parent</u>, and <u>Lead</u>*
- *The Miracle <u>Morning</u>: The 6 <u>Habits</u> that Will <u>Transform</u> Your Life Before 8 a.m.*
- *<u>Essentialism</u>: The <u>Disciplined</u> Pursuit of <u>Less</u>*

When you think you have your title and subtitle, ask yourself these two questions:

- Does my title/subtitle clearly convey what my book is about?
- Does my book title/subtitle contain search terms people looking for my book would be searching for?

If the answer to either of those questions is *no,* then keep brainstorming.

Cover

Your cover is your book's first impression. You absolutely must have a professional-looking cover, and DIY-ing it here is almost always a mistake. Consider the audience that will be purchasing your book. What would attract them? What kind of images and text? What words?

Book designer Jessica Freeman of Jess Creatives says, "We all judge a book by its cover, so don't underestimate the impact that your cover has to set the tone for your book! The best thing you can do is research other book covers, and see what grabs your attention." Looking at other covers not only helps you see what performs well in your genre (particular colors, fonts, types of art) but also helps you discern what you like/don't like in a cover. You can convey that information to your cover designer to make the design process smoother (because you're giving them a starting point).

If you simply cannot afford to hire someone to design your cover, keep in mind a few tips:

- Keep it simple.
- Choose a font that is readable (remember that the cover will be just a thumbnail on Amazon and on mobile devices) and a solid-color background.
- Be vigilant about copyright when choosing images.

As for graphics, if you are DIY-ing the cover, take a look at Etsy, Creative Market, and Haute Stock for ideas.

Nothing makes publishing more tangible than having a cover.
— Brooke Warner

Amazon has cover templates available, though I encourage you not to use them, or you might end up with the same cover as someone else (minus their title, of course). Your book deserves an original cover. There are affordable options like Fiverr and Upwork, though my clients have had good luck with 99designs.com and designing on Canva if they can't include a custom cover in their book budget.

Regardless of who designs your book cover, it should not be too busy. Make sure you include the following elements:
- Title and subtitle,
- Author,
- Image (optional),
- Testimonial (short; optional), and
- Starburst with short text (e.g., Foreword by ___; optional).

Also, remember that your cover also includes the spine and back cover.

The Cover Design Process

The process of finding a professional designer mirrors that of finding an editor. There are many out there, each with his or her own process. I asked a colleague for a recommendation and hired my cover designer after speaking with her briefly.

The process was straightforward (important for someone like me, who knows so little about design) and the communication was wonderful. She had me put images of covers I liked and didn't like in a project management software system, and I could include notes if I wanted (e.g., *I love the color of this cover but not the image*). She presented me with three choices initially, and we tweaked them until we found the cover of this book, which I love and which has been effective.

You'll want to know how many revisions are included in your contract and what the schedule/time line looks like.

Bar Codes

You need a bar code in addition to an ISBN. Why? Frankly, because the booksellers say so. In order to track inventory and sales, booksellers need a machine-readable, or scannable, version of the ISBN. The Bookland EAN symbol is the most widely used barcode format in the publishing industry. It encodes the ISBN and can also include the price. Large book retailers (and, though it does not matter to you directly, many book wholesalers) require books to display the Bookland EAN barcode graphic symbol, which carries the ISBN. Bar codes are placed at the bottom right corner of the back cover of a book.

Keep in mind that if you change the price after the bar code is produced, you will need a new bar code. Once a barcode is made, the price on it cannot be changed. (You can use the same ISBN on the new bar code because the book itself has not changed.)

You can purchase a bar code in a bundle with your ISBN, but check with your cover designer first. They may have a template they use, which will save you from purchasing one.

Action Steps

Remember that your cover and title are your book's first impression, so make it a good one!

- Consider the time-result formula when brainstorming titles.
- Use keywords that your audience will search for in your title and subtitle.
- Hire a cover designer if your budget allows.

Chapter 9
Publishing and Distribution

Are you planning to publish an ebook, a print book, or both? Will your print book be hardcover or paperback? My thought on this is simple: Don't limit yourself to just one platform. Make your words available to those who prefer print books as well as those who prefer to read on a tablet or device. I'm focusing on Amazon for publication because that's what nine out of 10 clients use, that's what I use, and that's what I imagine you will use.

> You can't change the world with a book that's still on your hard drive or in a box under your bed.
> — Joel Friedlander

Amazon Kindle Direct Publishing (KDP)

Why publish with Amazon? Let me count the reasons. . . . First and foremost, people go to Amazon to buy. They are on the site or mobile app to spend money. One of every five titles sold on Amazon, they say, is a Kindle book. So it's a no-brainer to have your book available there. Second, it's easy. The process is simple: Go to the KDP website (www.kdp.amazon.com), create an account, prepare your file to be uploaded, click "Create New Title," and enter your information. Your ebook will be available in the Kindle Store after a 24- to 48-hour wait. (Bonus: If you already have a print edition of the same book title on Amazon, Amazon will automatically link your books.)

When you provide the information for your book listing, give the book description special attention. The title/subtitle and cover will grab potential readers' attention, but a compelling book description is how you pull them in and convince them to buy the book. Readers use book descriptions to make purchasing decisions. Have you ever read back cover copy at a bookstore and thought either *Ooh—this sounds like just what I'm looking for!* or *Nope?* Julie Broad of Book Launchers urges authors to consider their book description "an advertisement, not a summary."

Another reason? Keywords (in your title and description) are among the factors that affect Amazon's algorithms. (Others are sales/conversion rates and having recent (verified) reviews.)

KDP Select

KDP Select is an exclusivity program. It allows you to earn higher royalties and reach a new audience (because your ebook will be available in many countries through Kindle Unlimited). KDP Select offers two promotional tools to authors: Kindle Countdown Deals, which is a time-bound promotional discounting of your book while you earn royalties, and Free Book Promotion, in which readers worldwide can get your book free for a limited time.

When you enroll your book in KDP Select, the digital format of your book is available exclusively (read: only) through KDP for 90 days. You may not sell your book digitally anywhere else (your website, your blog, another online bookseller, etc.) during the exclusivity period. (Be sure to read the KDP Select Terms and Conditions carefully for more details before committing.) Because of the exclusivity required, most of my clients don't enroll. The higher royalties are appealing, to be sure (when you publish on Amazon, you'll choose to keep either 70% or 35% of your royalties. The 70% option accompanies KDP Select.), but the exclusivity is a deal-breaker for many.

Paperbacks (and Other Print Editions)

One of the downsides of self-publishing in its early years was that authors ended up with boxes of books in their garages, basements, offices, and anywhere else they could think to store them, and they sold them (or not) from that supply. Today, there are many POD (print on demand) services, meaning that books are essentially not printed until they are demanded (AKA ordered). Authors aren't stuck with inventory—hurrah!

As with ebooks, Amazon is the biggest player for paperback books, though there are some others worth mentioning. In 2018, KDP and CreateSpace (Amazon's paperback publisher) "merged." Not too much changed, from an author-entrepreneur's perspective, other than royalty payouts, which are net 60 days (net 30 with CreateSpace) and keyword options (there are now more!).

KDP is a good choice if you're looking for a straightforward paperback book with black and white interior (no color).

The process is just like with uploading an ebook: Go to

the KDP website (www.kdp.amazon.com), create an account, prepare your file to be uploaded, click "Create New Title," and enter your information. The uploading process is simple and user-friendly, but if you're feeling unsure about DIY-ing this part of the process, check out author Dannie Fountain's video tutorial. (See the Resources.) Dannie has written and self-published multiple books and could probably become a millionaire by offering this service to author-entrepreneurs, frankly.

Amazon will sell books printed by a company other than KDP (IngramSpark is the one most author-entrepreneurs use) but note that they are listed on Amazon as out of stock for two weeks. This is how Amazon "encourages" authors to use their program.

You are not, of course, beholden to Amazon to print and distribute your book. Just as Amazon does, these services offer formatting and editing services in addition to publishing, at various price points:

- IngramSpark (www.ingramspark.com; good option for hardcover and paperback).
- Lulu (www.lulu.com; clients tell me Lulu is a good option for four-color books or coffee-table-sized books).
- BookBaby (www.bookbaby.com).
- Draft2Digital (www.draft2digital.com).
- Smashwords (www.smashwords.com).

With each of these service providers, you simply create an account and follow the steps to publish your book. Each is just a bit different, but the websites are, by and large, clear and user-friendly. If you use a hybrid publisher, you might have options regarding print runs, types of printing, and more.

Audio Books

Audio book production is becoming more and more friendly to self-publishing authors. It's also the fastest-growing segment of the book publishing industry, so I hope you're at least considering an audio book, even if you release it a bit later than your print/ebook versions. Audio books are great for readers who travel a lot or spend time on the go in general. (You'll know if you have such readers in your target market from the ideal reader exercise discussed in Chapter 1.)

Digital Printing Defined

Print on demand (POD; think KDP and Lulu) is essentially digital printing. This type of printing comes at a higher cost per unit, but there's no inventory to store. The quality of digital printing used to be inferior to offset and other types of printing used by publishing houses. (This is one reason self-publishing had such a bad name in the industry for so long.)

Distribution

You aren't finished making decisions once you select a publisher. Your book also needs to be distributed if you want anyone to buy it. You need a plan to get your book into booksellers (online and brick and mortar), libraries, and other, non-bookstore retail outlets.

Here's where it can get tricky. KDP is *not* a worldwide distributor (other than for Amazon). The largest and most well-known distributor in the book publishing world is Ingram. (IngramSpark is Ingram's printing and self-publishing arm.)

KDP does offer "expanded services," for which KDP uses Ingram to distribute the print book. Here's the key, though: It registers your book in the Ingram database with KDP as the publisher. This is true even if you use your own ISBN (versus the one CreateSpace can provide). You may be wondering, "But what does this mean for me?" Some booksellers (online and brick and mortar) think of Amazon as competition, and other booksellers still associate KDP with "indie" authors and won't carry books that list the publisher as KDP or are affiliated with Amazon.

Old habits die hard: The low quality that self-published books used to be known for is still fresh in some smaller bookstore owners' minds; whereas they can easily return unsold books to publishers and get their money back, it's trickier with self-published authors.

If you use IngramSpark directly, your books will appear to booksellers with your name as the publisher name.

So, yes, Amazon is a huge market. *But* consider this, from the IngramSpark website:

- Ingram has connections with more than 40,000 retailers and libraries worldwide.
- Ingram reaches the following channels, among others: Barnes & Noble, Apple, Kobo, and Amazon.

My point is this: Though Amazon is a behemoth, there are other places out there, and Ingram can help you reach them. Book buyers work through wholesalers, *not* through Amazon.

If you don't care about your book being in bookstores and/

or libraries, stick with KDP only. If you do, though, use In-gramSpark for your paperback and KDP for your ebook. I understand the temptation not to add another account to keep track of, but these are two distinct companies that provide different services for author-entrepreneurs.

When someone orders your book on Amazon, if Amazon finds you/your book via KDP, the customer receives the book without delay. It's immediately available. When Amazon finds you/your book via Ingram distribution, though, the book may not be listed as immediately available.

Libraries
For library distribution, you'll need CIP data (a Cataloging in Publication record). According to the Library of Congress website:

> The Cataloging in Publication program creates bib-liographic records for forthcoming books most likely to be widely acquired by U.S. libraries. The bibliographic record (also known as CIP data) is sent to the pub-lisher and printed on the verso of the title page. A ma-chine-readable version of the record is also distributed to libraries.

More and more libraries are housing ebooks, usually sup-plied by a company called OverDrive, so don't forget about libraries for your ebook, too.

Independent Bookstores
Plenty of independent bookstores shelve books by self-pub-lishing authors. Because shelf space is limited, though, you have to make it worthwhile. Here's how:

- Make your book returnable. Booksellers don't want

to be stuck with books they can't sell. (Traditional publishers allow booksellers to return unsold books.)

- Offer to host a book signing or other event at the store. In other words, show them that you have a plan to get foot traffic into their store.

Solo/Self-Distribution

If you have the means to handle sales and shipping, consider selling your book on your own website either in addition to other outlets or as your only means of distribution. My client Jessica Rasdall focused on direct selling for her book *Shattered* because one of her launch promos was "buy one for you and one for a friend," and she signed the books for the purchaser and their friend. It made sense to set up a direct sales channel. (Her book is available on Amazon, too, but she directs potential readers to the book page on her website, not the Amazon listing.)

Action Steps

Publishing and distributing are separate tasks that need an author's attention. Making decisions early ensures that you're ready to go when the book is finished.

- Determine which format(s) make sense for you to publish.
- Choose your distribution channels and set up accounts.

PART III: Market

_____

Chapter 10
Book Reviews

Truth be told, it can be a pain in the you-know-what to obtain book reviews. No author likes to ask for them. (It's like asking for a sale, in that if you don't do it the right way, it almost makes you feel icky. You are a business owner; you know what I'm talking about!) Once you get the first couple reviews to get the ball rolling, though, the snowball effect takes over, and you'll get more and more. There is no such thing as too many book reviews, especially if they're positive ones because then you can tailor them—segment them like you do your email lists. You might have a group of readers particularly interested in one aspect you cover in the book and another group interested in a different topic. For this book, for example, I expect to have readers interested in the whole process *as well as* readers only interested in either writing, publishing, or marketing.

Why You Need Reviews

What do you do with book reviews? Use them—*everywhere!* With an estimated 4,500 ebooks published daily, according to Amazon, you need to work to get your name out there. Reviews are one way to do that. On your author website, in your media kit and promo materials, in your email signature: Use reviews everywhere you can to promote your book, get your name out there, and help your book stand out in a saturated market.

Book reviews are important because they provide social proof, sure, but a lot of book promotion sites require them before they'll feature a book.

Getting Reviews

To get initial reviews and build buzz around your book launch, you need reviews—period. Make a list of 10 to 15 people to ask for reviews. Approach them to ask if you can send them a copy of your book before launch for them to read, provide feedback, and offer a review on Amazon. (You don't want too big of a list for this, because you also need and want people to buy your book!) Send the book four to six weeks before launch, and allow them at least a couple of weeks to read the book and post a review. Don't be surprised when you need to follow up. Send a note after a couple of weeks to check in. Ask how they like the book so far. Ask if there's anyone to whom they think you should send a link to your sales page.

Your review-gathering process does not need to be formal. Send a PDF of the book along with the cover, let them know it's not a final copy (so there could be a typo here and there or something wonky with the formatting), thank them in advance for their time, and give them a link to the book on Amazon so it's easy for them to leave a review when they are ready. The easier you can make the process, the more likely people will do it.

Once the book is published, if there are people who you

know have purchased your book, reach out to them via email or online informally in some other way to say, "I'd love to know what you think. I'm gathering some of my favorite book reviews, and I'd love to include one from you if you have the time to provide one. Book reviews are helpful for authors because they help books get noticed on Amazon. Just a couple of sentences would be wonderful. Thank you so much!" This is non-intimidating and casual, which is how you get people on board, and explaining how reviews are helpful is often that extra push people need. The people you approach want to see you succeed.

Amazon does not allow reviews before publication (though Goodreads and some other sites do), so a week or so before your launch, send an email to remind anyone who's received an advance copy of the launch date and that they can submit a review on that date. Include links to your Amazon and Goodreads pages to make it easy for them.

Remember Your Beta Readers?

The beta readers who had good things to say about your book might be willing to be early reviewers for you. Get in touch to thank them again and ask them to leave a review on Amazon if they wouldn't mind. Your beta readers are already invested in you and your book. They want you to succeed, so they are great people to ask for a review.

Media Reviews

Media outlets each have a process you need to follow to get a book reviewed. If there is a particular publication you're interested in, go to their website and check their submissions guidelines. Remember that the bigger the publication, the longer the lead time, so if you're submitting a book a month or two before publication, you're likely months too late for national publications. (A virtual assistant who does publicity work can help you formulate a plan of where you want to submit for review.)

Consider the following media outlets as you start to build your wish list:

- Kirkus,
- Netgalley,
- *Publisher's Weekly,* the go-to book publishing magazine for industry professionals,
- Industry publications (magazines, association newsletters, and the like), websites, and blogs,
- General interest publications like Buzzfeed, Huffington Post, and Thrive Global, and
- Business publications like *Inc., Fast Company, Wired, Business Week.*

When you get media reviews, you use them the same way you do any other review: promote, promote, promote! Often industry reviews are paid reviews, so don't get sticker shock when you start researching in this area.

Other Review Sources

Don't forget to send copies of the book to any people or companies who are mentioned. Surely they'll want to help spread the word. Also consider media professionals and influencers in your industry.

Remember that a review from anyone who works on your book and is compensated (such as your editor and cover designer) violates Amazon's policies.

Action Steps

Reviews are important for social proof and are a great marketing tool for you as an author. There is no such thing as too many book reviews.

- Create a list of people to approach to ask for a review.
- Build a list of publications to which to submit your book for review.

Chapter 11
Launching and Book Marketing

Without a marketing strategy, your book will sit on Amazon gathering figurative dust. If you build it, they will come? Not in a saturated book market. Start by crafting a launch plan. You can do this yourself, you can hire a virtual assistant or project manager to help with/manage this, or you can hire a book marketing specialist or book publicist. Your choice will depend on how much time you can devote to marketing (before *and* after launch), whether or not marketing is a specialty of yours (something you do regularly in your business), and your budget.

A quick note about hiring a professional: They can surely lighten your workload when it comes to book marketing, but as the author, you will always have marketing work to do. And hiring someone does not guarantee media coverage, placement in certain publications, or increased sales.

Marketing is merely looking to connect with readers so you can add value to their lives.
— Tim Grahl

As a business owner, your launch plan is two-pronged: You're marketing in the traditional ways, as you would any other launch in your business, to your warm audience—but you're also marketing via book distribution to a cold audience.

A launch plan for anything (course, product, website—you name it) has a lot of moving pieces. You *must* be organized. Your first task is to pick a launch date—a specific date, not "sometime this fall" or "right after Christmas." Between six and nine months seems to be the sweet spot for most business owners. Less than that and there's just too much to be done, and more than that allows you to procrastinate because you think you have "plenty of time." Setting a date and announcing it, whether publicly on one of your social media accounts, or privately to your accountability partner or mastermind group, will help keep you accountable. (You hate to disappoint others, right?)

Every launch plan looks different. You may include activities and tasks that aren't mentioned here—and you may skip some that are. Do what feels right for you and your book. This chapter includes elements and tasks that I regularly see in launch plans, and that seem to work well for most of my author-entrepreneur clients.

Organizing Your Launch Plan

The organization of your launch plan will be personal preference but also depend on who else needs access to your plan. You can keep your plan on a calendar (written or online), or you can put it in a task-management program and share with team members. (I use Trello for mine, and my VA has access to launch related and ongoing marketing tasks that require her attention.) Remember what I noted earlier in the book when discussing research: *What* system you use is less important than simply *having* a system. The same principle applies here. Use what works for you, but use something to keep all of the moving pieces in working order.

Marketing Time Line

The longevity a book offers is part of its marketing appeal. It's never too early to start marketing your book, and essentially you never stop. I know, I know: That sounds exhausting. Like book writing, though, book marketing is a marathon and not a sprint. You will earn income from your book for as long as it's available for purchase. But you will earn *more* income from your book—and reach more people—if you keep marketing it in some way. Your *big* launch activities will come when the book is first released—in the weeks leading up to launch, on launch day, and in the immediate weeks following release. Some ideas for promotions long after launch, though, include re-releasing your book with a new cover, updated reviews, and maybe a few updated statistics; adding a chapter or a new foreword; and holding an anniversary sale.

> Marketing starts even before our books are published.
> — Heather Hart

Most marketing tasks don't have a set time frame in which they *must* be done, though a few do. If you're doing a pre-sale, for example, you should set that up three to four weeks before your release (launch date). Anything that requires set-up time should be scheduled carefully, but most of your tasks can be completed in your order of preference.

> The most efficient marketing is consistent marketing.
> — Shelley Hitz

Start building your launch plan early so that you can add to it and adjust as needed. Any time you have some extra time (I know: ha!), complete a task. Can you set aside two hours one morning each week for the two months leading up to your launch to work on launch activities? Would it work better for you to take 30 minutes each morning? Just like your writing schedule, the logistics of your book marketing activities will depend on your existing day-to-day routine. As soon as you are finished writing, though, turn your attention to marketing. You'll have blocks of time when the manuscript is with beta readers, then with an editor, then with a designer that can be filled (and then some) with launch and marketing activities.

Social Media: Educate Your Audience Before You Launch

While you're writing and before you launch, you should be educating your audience and building your email list. You do this with value-filled blog posts, webinars, social media posts, videos, and so forth. Update old blog posts related to your book topic and that were popular. Write guest posts to get yourself in front of new audiences. Find other collaboration partners. If you're on Pinterest, create a Pinterest graphic for your lead magnet that links to the landing page for your book. Do a

Facebook, Instagram, or YouTube Live series before launch to invite people to sign up for book updates. Tease what's coming in the weeks before your book launches. Mention it in your email newsletter. Plan complementary content everywhere to continue to establish yourself as a trusted expert for your audience. (This is likely something you're already doing. If not, there's no better time to start.)

Hashtag Heaven

As you're writing and working on your launch plan, start building a hashtag library with hashtags that are book-related, writing-related, and topic-related. Use these as a starting point:

> #amwriting
> #selfpublishing
> #amediting
> #indiebooks
> #authorlife
> #writerslife
> #bookauthor
> #getpublished
> #pubday

Think of others, too. Maybe you'll post a teaser from the book every Tuesday and use #teasertuesday or #teasertues. Maybe you'll post a picture of your computer screen and use #wordcount or #wip (work in progress). Definitely use your book title as a hashtag, too. Instagram allows 30 hashtags per post as of this writing (May 2019). Use them!

Email Sequences

Decide how many emails you'll send as part of your launch.

Your emails should show the value of your book; help readers overcome objections to purchasing and show how the book can help your audience reach their goals. As always, don't hard-sell in every email in the sequence.

Though the emails will be sent in the days leading up to launch day, you can (and should) batch write and schedule them well in advance. The closer launch day gets, the busier you will be, so having this task checked off early will be a huge bonus for you.

Book Website or Sales Page

Do you want a website solely for your book (or for you as an author)? Or will you have a dedicated page on your existing website? Both options work. If you want to build a brand as an author—separate from your business—then it makes sense to have a website for your books. A book website should include these pages at a minimum:

- Book cover and description,
- Praise/testimonials,
- A Look Inside (sample chapter, contents, etc.),
- About the Author (bio and headshot),
- Media Kit, and
- Events.

Of course, you can include much more, but this list should be the starting point. Include links to purchase on each page, and be sure the site is optimized for mobile viewing.

Regardless of which option you choose for your web presence, if you aren't a designer, hire one so that your page looks professional. There's a lot of information to include, including graphics, and the last thing you want is a non-user-friendly, cluttered website. Make it easy for people to learn about you and your book (not to mention easy to purchase it!). If you decide to build a new website for your book, remember to budget both the time and expense.

If you choose to have a dedicated sales page on your existing site, include the following information:

- Cover image,
- Reasons to buy (reader benefits),
- Reviews/praise,
- Links to interviews/events,
- Links to purchase,
- Sample chapter,
- Author bio/headshot,
- Book description, and
- Book trailer (if you have one).

Your goal is to include anything a potential reader would want so that they only need to click once to leave the page—and that's to purchase the book from an online retailer.

Media Kit

You'll use your media kit throughout your book launch and beyond. Prepare the following, so you have these elements ready to send when asked to submit them:

- Long book summary,
- Short book summary,
- Book title, subtitle, tagline,
- Book cover,
- Book info sheet: ISBN, price, categories, availability date, links to purchase,
- Long author bio,
- Short author bio,
- Headshot(s),

- Sample Q&A (Make it easy for guest bloggers and others to promote your book!),
- Press release, and
- Social media share templates (images and copy).

Consider setting up an email address for anything related to book marketing (e.g., info@booktitle.com or hello@booktitle.com). This will keep you organized during a hectic book launch because you won't have to search multiple places. Anything related will be in that one inbox.

To Pre-Sell or Not to Pre-Sell

Authors have *vastly* differing opinions on whether or not to offer a pre-sale—and whether or not to offer discounted pricing if you do. Some authors prefer instead to offer bonuses for people who buy during the pre-sale period instead of a discounted price. If you decide a pre-sale is right for you, set up your Amazon accounts to allow for it. KDP does not directly allow pre-sales for paperbacks, so you set up an Amazon Advantage account (advantage.amazon.com) to handle paperback pre-sales. (It's not complicated; it's essentially just another log-in and password to keep track of.) If you do a pre-sale, don't forget to remove it before your book launches, especially if you're offering it at a lower price during pre-sale.

Launch Ambassadors/Cheerleaders

Launch ambassadors are people who will celebrate your launch by sharing it with their audience and cheering you on. Think of 15–20 people who might be willing. Email them with a cover image, the table of contents, and a sample chapter you think might interest them. Ask if they would be willing to celebrate your launch with you. Not everyone will be willing/interested or able, and that's okay. Get as many people on board as you can. You can ask for launch ambassadors in Facebook groups you belong to as well.

When someone agrees to be a launch ambassador, first and foremost thank them. Also, make it easy for them: Prepare images and social media captions as well as email newsletter copy they can use to share the launch. Let them know when they can (and shouldn't) share. The easier you can make this for people, the likelier it is that they will follow through.

Live Events

The sooner you can make a connection with potential readers, the better the chance of them making a purchase. That obviously cannot happen on Amazon (though it *can* happen on your website with your book trailer), but it sure can at live events. Schedule book signings at local booksellers and other retailers/companies. If you've published a cookbook, get in touch with kitchen stores and grocery stores. If you've written a marketing book, reach out to local small businesses and networking groups like chambers of commerce. If you've published a gardening book, reach out to nurseries and flower stores. Offer to host a reading and discussion at your library. Contact business organizations and offer to speak at a lunch and learn. Fill out speaker submissions for conferences and workshops in your industry. Get in front of your potential readers.

Make sure you have enough books available at live events for people to purchase. Bookstores typically take care of this for you, but if you are speaking at a conference or to a group, generally authors supply their books themselves.

Promo Items

If you plan to do any in-person events, such as book signings or speaking, think about whether or not you want to have an item to give away in addition to selling your book. Some authors have pens or postcards with the book cover, but think outside the box here (but with your budget in mind). You are limited only by your imagination and your budget. I have worked with an author of a wellness and self-care book who ordered all-natural lip balm, a cookbook author who ordered small spatulas for a demo she did, and a sales book author who handed out flash drives at every conference where she spoke. If you do want swag, allow plenty of time for design and shipment.

Also, consider whether or not your events are local. You wouldn't want to ship, say, 100 coffee mugs to a conference where you'll be speaking. One, they're heavy so the shipping cost would be substantial, and two, they're fragile. Have these sorts of things shipped directly to the conference site—or consider an alternate item.

Giveaways

Giveaways are a fun way to drum up enthusiasm for your book. You can, of course, give away the traditional items: Kindle e-reader, Amazon gift card, Starbucks gift card. But think of non-traditional prizes, too. If your book is about photography, maybe you could give away a camera bag. If that's not in your budget, what about a camera strap or an "Editing Day" coffee mug? If your book is about entrepreneurship, the sky is the limit as far as swag: prints, coffee mugs, shirts—you name it, and you can find a quote about entrepreneurship. You could also do a digital subscription to a publication.

Reviews

I won't lie: This part is no fun. Lots of people will promise to leave a review on Amazon and then won't follow through. Book reviews are a *huge* source of traffic to your book or ebook, so you must ask for them—early and often—throughout your launch and beyond. Many readers use reviews as a driving force when deciding whether or not to purchase a book. (I covered reviews in detail in Chapter 10, so just a quick reminder here, as reviews definitely play a critical role in your launch.)

BookBub Feature Deal

Maybe you've heard of BookBub, from a reader's standpoint. If you haven't, check it out. BookBub is a site that offers discount Kindle books daily. As a reader, you can sign up for deals by interest/genre, and each day you get an email with deals for the day. As an author, you can submit your book for a "Feature Listing." Yes, the one-time cost is high, depending on the discounted price you'll set, but the return can be remarkable. As of May 2019, BookBub lists 600,000+ subscribers to the business category. To have BookBub list your ebook free, the one-time cost is $258. To have your ebook discounted to less than $1, the cost is $375. To have your book discounted between $1 and $2, the cost is $642, and to have your ebook discounted at a price higher than $2, the one-time cost is $935. BookBub also lists the average downloads based on their historical data:

- Average number of downloads (free business ebooks): 7,600

- Average number sold (discounted business ebooks): 890

So consider the up-front cost versus the return. That's *a lot* of books to give away for free—but can you get good reviews from some of those to use in further marketing campaigns? Are 890 sales enough to improve your Amazon ranking? Consider these questions when thinking about whether or not to add this into your launch plan.

Book Trailers

A book trailer is, essentially, a commercial for your book. Common particularly among fiction books, they are growing in popularity among nonfiction books. Think of a book trailer as you would a brand video on your website: you talking on screen and then voice over showing your office, your products—something along those lines. Book trailers are just a couple of minutes long. Book trailers start with the same premise but focus on your book rather than on you. You might start with a shot of the cover of the book, then you talking about the book and how it came to be/why you're the right person to write the book, and then you can get creative. Maybe show an interior page spread if you have images. Or you working with a client if you're a service-based business. Or you performing your work, whether that be photography, book editing, coaching—you get the idea.

Video is a largely untapped market when it comes to nonfiction books. The power of video cannot be overstated. What do these stats from ComScore tell you about whether or not you should take the time to make a book trailer:

- Visitors to your site stay an average of two minutes longer if your site uses video.
- Readers are 64% more likely to purchase your book if they see a trailer that effectively promotes your book.

One more stat, this one from Forrester Research: Open rates for authors who use video in an email campaign increase from 19 to 300%.

Don't be intimidated by video. You can produce a high-quality video with good natural lighting and your camera phone. Video is remembered more than text and images combined—*combined!*—so this one is really a no-brainer.

Amazon and Goodreads Listings

When you set up your book listing on Amazon for pre-order, Amazon assigns your book an ASIN (basically, Amazon's internal ID for your book). Take note of this number, because you need it to set up your Goodreads (www.goodreads.com) listing. Note that, while Amazon does not allow reviews until a book is launched, Goodreads does. So the sooner this listing is active, the sooner you can begin collecting reviews.

Though it won't take the place of your website, an Amazon Central Author Page is a tool you want to utilize. Think of it as another social media profile. People who find you through an Amazon search (and that's really what Amazon is: a search engine) will be able to learn more about you. Maybe your book shows up as a "Customers also bought" when someone makes a purchase. This could be someone who would never found you otherwise. Add your bio and a photo at a minimum. Many of these people will never visit your website, so make use of this Amazon Author Page.

Before you think you can skip the Amazon Central page as an author-entrepreneur rather than a professional writer planning to write multiple books, remember that your Amazon marketing is for the audience who *doesn't* know you. Your business friends, your family, and your clients already know how to find you (and how great you are). This is for those people who don't (yet).

Action Steps

Book marketing requires you, as an author, to play the short game leading up to and during your launch—as well as the long game post-launch.

- Set your marketing budget.
- Create a launch plan with activities prioritized according to your budget.

Conclusion

What do you think? Are you ready to cross "write a book" off your business bucket list? I hope *Write.Publish.Market.* has convinced you that the process does not have to be overwhelming (or take a decade!).

Happy writing!

Glossary of Book Publishing Terms

Welcome to the world of book publishing, where we sometimes speak our own language! This glossary should help you feel like an industry insider.

Acknowledgments: the recognition given to those who have assisted or influenced the book being published; the section of a book containing such recognition.

Advance: payment made as an advance against royalties by a publisher when an author's book is acquired by a traditional publisher; the advance is charged against royalties and must "earn out" (that is, royalties must total the amount of the advance) before any royalties are paid to an author.

Appendix: supplemental information at the end of a book, which can include tables and statistical information, case studies, samples, and more.

Author Biography: personal information about the author, including education, professional achievements, and publications.

Back Matter: any material that appears in the back of the book following the body copy, such as appendixes, endnotes, references, glossary, or index.

Back-of-the-Room Sales: author sales made at an event. (Often when an author speaks at a conference, the author's books are for sale, usually at a table at the back of the conference room.)

Bibliography: a list of books or articles used by the author in preparing his or her work; sources may or may not be cited directly.

Binding: the back cover, spine, and front cover of a book.

Blurb: the brief description of a book that appears on the back of a paperback or on the inside front flap of a hardcover book.

Book Signing: an event featuring an author reading from/ discussing his or her book and/or autographing copies of the book for customers.

Copy Editor: the line editor of a manuscript whose goal is to correct grammar and mechanical inconsistencies, ensure consistency of tone and voice, and ensure clarity and readability.

Copyright: ownership of intellectual property.

Copyright Page: a page in the front matter indicating that the book is protected by copyright and that permission must be obtained to reproduce all or part of the book.

Developmental Editor: the editor who addresses the "big picture" of the book with regard to organization, structure, and content; often the first step in the formal editing process.

Distributor: a company that sells to retailers (instead of directly to consumers).

EAN Bar Code: the machine-readable form of the ISBN which is encoded with information such as the title, publisher, and price.

Ebook: electronic book.

Endorsement: a promotional statement by someone recommending a book.

Epigraph: a short quotation or saying at the beginning of a book or chapter.

Foreword: an introduction to a book written by someone other than the author.

Front Matter: the pages in a book that appear before the body copy, including the title page, copyright page, dedication, table of contents, foreword, preface, acknowledgments, and introduction.

Genre: the broad category of book (e.g., romance, business, sci-fi, self-help, true crime)

Half-Title Page: the first page of a book, on which just the book title is displayed.

Index: an alphabetical list of words that guides a reader to the specific pages on which the subject appears in the body of the book.

International Standard Book Number (ISBN): the unique 13-digit number (10 or 13 digits prior to 2007) that identifies a version of a book.

Keyword: word (or phrase) searched to find related results for a subject area.

List Price: the cover price of a book; also called the retail price.

Manuscript: the author's complete written version of a book.

Media Kit: promotional materials used to announce

information to the news media and other outlets; also called press kit.

Metadata: data about data (in this case about your book; e.g., title, author, ISBN, category).

Online Retailer: bookstore on the Web that sells to consumers.

Permissions: agreement from a copyright holder granting the right to someone else to reproduce the work.

Preface: introductory section of a book, usually written by the author, explaining why the book was written or how to use the book.

Print-on-Demand (POD): publishing model in which books are printed only as orders are placed.

Print-Ready: final PDF files of a book that are ready to go to the printer.

Print Run: the number of copies of a book that are printed.

Proofreader: the editor who does the final proof of a typeset manuscript.

Public Domain: work that is not legally protected as

intellectual property or whose protection has expired is in the public domain; no permissions required to use material/words in the public domain.

Publication Date: the official date when a book is released to the public; also called launch date.

Royalty: payment made to an author; usually a percentage of sales revenue.

Self-Publishing: method of book publishing in which the author assumes the financial risk of publication and is responsible for all aspects of publication.

Sell Sheet: a concise, one-page document providing details about a book.

Table of Contents: list of a book's contents with their opening page numbers.

Target Audience: the specific group of people a book is marketed to; also called target market.

Title Page: page displaying the book title, author, and publisher.

Traditional Publishing: the business model for publishing books in which a publishing house contracts with authors who write books, edits and prepares it for printing or electronic publishing, has it printed, and then markets/distributes it; also called trade publishing and mainstream publishing.

Trim Size: the final physical dimensions of a book page after the book is bound and trimmed.

Typesetting: the process of formatting a book on a computer, resulting in the layout, font, and appearance on a printed page.

Resources

IBPA Industry Standards Checklist for a Professionally Published Book
Independent Book Publishers Association
https://www.ibpa-online.org/page/standardschecklist

How to Publish on Amazon
https://www.danniefountain.com/buynow/how-to-publish-on-amazon

How to Print a Book with IngramSpark
https://www.ingramspark.com/blog/how-to-create-a-print-book?utm_content=88184704&utm_medium=social&utm_source=facebook&hss_channel=fbp-103517499839099&fbclid=IwAR2uSTZHEg3kz6y06UkxX_wOncgNLYplV4694r_Qzdq1ITbcy-vnM65nde8

The Book Designer
www.thebooksdesigner.com

Jane Friedman
https://www.janefriedman.com/

BookBub
www.bookbub.com

BookBub Feature Deal Pricing
https://www.bookbub.com/partners/pricing

U.S. Copyright Office
https://www.copyright.gov/registration/

Book Industry Study Group
http://bisg.org/page/BISACSubjectCodes

Index

J

K

L

P

R

About the Author

After 20 years in traditional book publishing, book writing/ publishing coach and editor Jodi Brandon's passion these days is helping creative and online entrepreneurs scale their business with a self-published book. Jodi leverages her industry experience to help small business owners and entrepreneurs publish a high-quality, professional book—and has helped hundreds of business owners do just that. She lives outside of Philadelphia with her husband, Dave, and their rescue dog, JoePa.

CPSIA information can be obtained
at www.ICGtesting.com
Printed in the USA
LVHW051425071019
633402LV00003B/909/P